The Retreat
Stephanie Hazeltine

THE RETREAT

Edited: Mel Noorderbroek at Write On Editorial

Cover design: The Cover Collection

Published by Hazeltine Publishing

Ebook: 978-0-6455756-6-8

Paperback: 978-0-6455756-7-5

For Mum,

The strongest woman I know

Prologue

C elia brings the bottle of sparkling wine to her lips, completely unaware of the people watching her. The weekend didn't go as planned and now she's left with no choice but to implement damage control. Whether or not she's a lost cause, she doesn't know. And right now, alcohol seems like the best answer.

The door to her room creaks open. 'Megan?' she calls out, but there's no response.

That doesn't bother Celia. Megan is in damage control too. She probably has no desire to talk to Celia right now.

Grabbing a fresh bottle, Celia stumbles onto her balcony. She pops the top off and paces. She talks to herself as she walks back and forth, racing over the events of the past few days.

A strange feeling makes her stop and she stares out into the shrubbery that stands between her room and the beach. The view would be breathtaking in different circumstances. She's certain she's seen or heard something, but there's nothing there. She blames the wine before heading back inside.

It's dark and Celia's about to call it a night. She takes one last look out the back door to the bushes and beach beyond. And then it hits her.

The force of the push knocks her to the floor and her head whips back as it makes contact with the sharp edge of the coffee table.

That's the last thing she remembers as her eyes close, while lying in a pool of her own blood.

A Lifesaver for Our Relationship!

Excerpt of Google Review for Celia Marsden Therapy Services

June, 2010

I can't express how grateful my partner and I are for finding such an amazing couples therapist in Celia. Our journey through relationship struggles led us to her and she truly transformed our lives for the better.

From our very first session, it was evident that Celia possessed an exceptional level of empathy. She made us feel heard and understood without judgement, creating a safe space where we could openly discuss our issues. Her warm and approachable demeanour immediately put us at ease, making it easy to open up about our concerns.

Chapter 1

Celia

I calmly place my hand on the counter. 'Do you know who I am?' My eyes narrow in on the young woman behind the desk. Her name badge reads Tammy.

She's typing away at her computer at a frantic speed. She looks up at me. 'I do apologise, Ms Marsden, but there doesn't seem to be a booking under your name.'

'We can just get a cab, it doesn't matter,' my friend, Kitty, calls from behind me.

I shoot her a look that I hope conveys my shock. I do not travel in regular cabs. Not anymore.

'My manager, Megan, booked a private transfer in one of your luxury vehicles. If you've made a mistake on your end, that's not my problem. Please arrange for one of your drivers to pick us up, now.'

'Ms Marsden, there are no cars avail—'

The young woman is cut off by a man working at the computer beside her. He's just finished with a customer.

'Celia Marsden, it is a pleasure to have you travel with us. Tammy, why don't you see if Lucien is available?'

'But—' Tammy attempts to protest.

'He's just outside.' He smiles at her, eyes wide. The expression you give someone when you want to say, *don't ask questions, just do it.* I've become somewhat used to this kind of interaction. I have a way of making people do exactly what I want them to do.

'Thank you,' I say, pursing my lips before turning to Kitty. 'Won't be long.'

She rolls her eyes. 'You know there's nothing wrong with getting a cab, Ceels?'

'Your best friend doesn't sell over a million copies of her book so that she can travel like a pleb.'

'I've seen you make out with a random guy from a bar in the back of a cab and if I remember correctly, you lost your underwear in that car.' Kitty flicks her long dark hair behind one shoulder, an act of victory.

I scowl at her before looking around to make sure no one heard her. 'I was nineteen. That's almost twenty years ago. A lot has changed.'

'Apparently,' she says under her breath, but loud enough for me to hear.

Kitty has been my best friend since high school but at times I wonder if she's envious of my success. We both went to university and studied psychology but my path took a very different turn five years ago and our friendship has been different ever since.

'Just remember who invited you to this retreat, Kitty Kat.' I use the pet name I know she loathes.

'Only because you didn't want to come on your own.'

I'm about to bite back when Tammy returns to the desk.

'Ms Marsden, your car is waiting for you out the front. Our driver, Lucien, will meet you at the exit. Safe travels.' She smiles but I can tell behind that look, she's saying, *now get out of my face, bitch.* And that's fine. I have that effect on people. But if said people did their jobs properly, we wouldn't have a problem.

A man waits by the door holding a piece of paper with my name freshly scribbled onto it. He looks to be in his mid-forties and wears a suit. The professional attire is very out of place at Ballina Airport, especially in this heat. However, it is what I expect in a chauffeur, so I'm pleased that he'll be the one to take us to the resort just south of Byron Bay.

I slide into the backseat next to Kitty while Lucien loads our cases into the trunk of the car. Scoffing loudly, I look at Kitty in disgust. 'What is that?'

'What?' she asks, shrugging her narrow shoulders. She's always had such a tiny frame. I have to work hard for my figure and she doesn't have to do anything. *Money can't buy everything.*

'That smell? What perfume are you wearing?'

'I just sprayed some YSL. You bought it for me last Christmas.'

I scrunch up my face. 'I don't think that's your scent, honey. It doesn't pair well with your natural odour.'

'Wow, Celia. Are you stressed about this retreat or are you becoming more of a bitch each day for no reason?'

I sigh. 'Sorry,' I say, even though I can't help it if her scent is suffocating me in the confined space of the car. 'I'm not stressed though. I just really can't be bothered with this retreat. I should never have agreed to it.'

'Well, why did you?'

'Megan said I need to stay relevant or I may risk losing my following.'

'Oh, because you're an *influencer* now.' She drags out the word influencer, mocking me.

'We'll see how you feel about my influencer status when you're sitting by the pool in a few hours holding a cocktail—free of charge.'

'Touché,' she responds. 'So what is the plan for the weekend anyway?'

'Nothing for you. You can just live it up eating, drinking and doing all the activities.'

Kitty's face lights up. She hasn't had a holiday in years. After having her kids, she and her husband have been working full time. They live comfortably enough but can't afford to save for a holiday.

'To be honest, I'm just excited to sleep and not hear the word "Mum" called out every two minutes. What will you be doing?' she asks.

'Counselling sessions with couples and singles, book readings.' I shudder at the thought of it all. I haven't done a face-to-face therapy session in a long time. I've been riding the success of my book for so long that I haven't had to practise psychology in a while. At first, I missed it. It is, or perhaps was, my passion. But I grew fond of the book events and the flexibility of promoting material on my own terms and in my own time.

'Returning to the therapist's chair, hey? Welcome back.'

'You might need to give me some pointers,' I say. When Kitty and I graduated with psychology degrees, I focused on couples therapy and she went into general psychology.

'Well, you can start by not telling your patients that they smell.'

I smile. 'Well, here's hoping they don't.'

Chapter 2

Molly

I glance at my watch. It's just after midday—less than two hours until the guests begin to arrive for the retreat and I don't feel prepared at all.

Why did I sign up for this?

Sure, Celia Marsden has the potential to put the Sand & Salt Resort on the map and make it famous. But she also has the power to destroy us.

I started managing the resort in northern New South Wales three years ago. The owners are never around and they don't really care what I do as long as the place turns a profit. Unfortunately, it's not doing as well as they'd like and I've felt the pressure to make some changes. I'm sure the owners wouldn't think twice about replacing me if their profits dropped. But I can't lose this job. This job is not just an income, it's a place to live. Without it, I'll be living in a bungalow at the back of my parents' house. Forty, single, unemployed and living with my parents. It can't happen.

You'd think because every second celebrity and influencer is moving to Byron Bay that the town, and its surrounds, would be a hot spot to visit. And it is. But it also means that every other person with some extra cash owns a fancy AirBnB or trendy, organic-food-only, yoga-everyday resort. Sand & Salt, while beautiful, is only one of many and isn't on many people's radar, or Instagram feeds.

So, in a panic, I reached out to Celia Marsden to float the idea of a weekend retreat. A weekend for married couples to work on their relationships and fresh singles who want to find themselves after their divorce. To be honest, I couldn't care less what they're doing here for the weekend as long Celia posts a few glowing reviews on her Instagram page. Sand & Salt could certainly use a little love from her 680,000 followers.

Yep. She's huge.

Therapist, turned author, turned influencer.

Her book, *Loveless Marriage,* has sold over a million copies worldwide. Personally, I've never read it but apparently it has saved marriages all over the world. However, for every couple that dedicates their marriage to Celia, another dedicates their divorce. Celia Marsden gave women all over the planet permission to leave their husbands. I'm sure as a couples therapist that was not her original intention, but she's profited from the phenomenon and she loves to toot her own horn about how she's empowering women. *Ugh. Whatever.* Just let this weekend go well.

Greg enters the dining area where I'm frantically folding napkins into fancy shapes, which, let's be real, no one cares about. I hate how calm he looks. He hasn't been losing sleep about this weekend. Sure, there's not as much pressure on him but it'd be nice if he pretended to be stressed to make me feel better.

'Alright, so all the guest rooms are clean and ready. Gardens are tidy and the pool is sparkling.' He finishes his sentence with a little, mocking bow.

I can't help but smile. 'Thank you.'

'What else can I do?' he asks.

Greg's role at Sand & Salt is technically security. But due to our lull in guests, he helps out everywhere. The two women in housekeeping love when he joins them to clean the rooms. Pretty much everyone loves it when he joins them anywhere because he's the laid-back larrikin who makes them all laugh. He wears the same thing every day—navy cargo shorts and a polo shirt in the same colour with the white Sand & Salt logo on it. The shirt hugs a round pot belly and shows the skin on his arms, which have years of sun damage from outdoor work. At fifty-years-old, Greg is like an older brother to me. Nothing gets to him and he calms me down.

'Can you wake me up when she leaves?' I sigh.

'When does Queen Celia arrive?' He puts on a posh English accent and I shove him.

'Don't,' I say, eyes wide. 'We need this to go well. No jokes.'

Greg rolls his eyes.

'She arrives at two,' I add. 'Can you please go and run through all the dietary requirements with Carlos again?'

Carlos is an incredible chef but he likes to get caught up in the moment, cooking whatever his *heart is feeling*, or so he tells me. I'm worried his heart may be feeling seafood when Celia specifically said the smell of fish makes her vomit.

'Yep, I'll come back to greet the queen,' he winks at me, 'and the guests at two.'

Greg leaves the dining room and I can't help but feel grateful for having him here.

I finish folding the napkins and take one last glance around the dining room. Sand & Salt was a school camp in the nineties. The owners bought it in the early 2000's and turned it into a luxury resort—although what counts for luxury in 2002 doesn't quite cut it in the influencer world of 2023. Some of the spaces still scream school camp and the dining room is one of them. I can just imagine sixty adolescents devouring mass-produced spaghetti Bolognese at trestle tables in this room. I hope my fancy napkins and skilled chef hide the room's history from the retreat guests.

I decide to do one last check of the deluxe suites—one of which will be accommodating Queen Celia. *Dammit, Greg.* Celia's friend, whom she demanded get the other suite, is also joining us for the weekend. And because she's Celia's friend, she isn't paying. That's how it works with these people. Now my two most expensive rooms are spending the weekend adding no money to the bottom line. Celia and this friend of hers better get *influencing* or whatever they call it.

The deluxe suites are next to one another at the far end of the resort overlooking the ocean. Both of their back balconies face the beach and have recently had small jacuzzis installed. The rooms have a fully stocked bar fridge, drinks are complimentary. There's a grand king-sized bed with the softest sheets you can possibly imagine, a sofa facing an enormous television and an ensuite with incredible marble tiling and one of those huge showers with a showerhead at each end.

Celia's room looks great. A bottle of Veuve is on ice waiting for her, along with a welcome basket of goodies—fresh pastries, fruit and chocolate. I fluff a few pillows and then head back to reception via the pool area. Greg was right, the pool is sparkling. Lounges line two sides of the pool, complete with bright cushions. A small shed sits at one end of the pool. It used to be the lifeguard's station when the kids came for camp. Now it houses our water toys—stand up paddle boards, snorkel gear, surf boards. We've got it all.

When I get back to reception it's ten past one. *Where has the time gone?* The reception building is two-storey and I live on the second floor. On one hand, it's handy living close to work but it also means I'm always here and the staff and guests know it. I rarely get a day off.

I head upstairs for a shower and to get into something more professional. Most people don't mind my usual attire of flowy skirts and bright colours—"it's a vibe" they say. But I have a feeling Celia has a very different vibe.

Chapter 3

Jocelyn

'O-M-G, Andy, did you see who that was?' I'm trying to keep my excitement to a whisper.

'No,' he says unenthusiastically and looks in the same direction as me.

'That was Luke Hemsworth. In the flesh. I can't wait to tell Hannah when I get home.' Hannah is my best friend and fellow Hemsworth lover. I prefer Chris, she prefers Liam but let's face it, we wouldn't say no to any of them, including Luke. I crane my neck to see where he's going but he disappears from sight.

I bop up and down on my feet watching the baggage carousel send bag after bag past me. Patience is not my strong suit, especially when there are Hemsworths to spot.

'What is wrong with you?' Andy asks. His dark eyes narrow, judging me. He looks so hot in his white t-shirt and chino shorts. His dark skin is smooth, except on his face where he has dark stubble along his jawline. He could be a movie star himself, or model, or influencer, although he loathes social media.

'I'm just so excited. A whole weekend with Celia Marsden. Plus, we're right near Byron Bay; we could see so many celebrities this weekend.'

Andy rolls his eyes. 'Remember why we're here, Joss,' he says, his tone serious.

I really hate when he speaks to me like a child. Of course I know why we're here. Andy and I have been together for ten years. We got married three years ago and it was beautiful. But the moment we said, "I do" our parents were on our backs about babies.

'You're not getting any younger, Jocelyn,' Mum had said, even though I was only twenty-nine.

'When will you give me a grandbaby?' Andy's mum asked, as though it was as simple as asking what time it is.

Andy and I have always wanted kids and just over a year ago we started "trying". I use the apps, I check my temperature, I pee on sticks and I even dress up sometimes to make it a little spicier when the scheduled sex becomes a chore. However, we've had no luck.

It's taken a toll on our relationship. "We're trying" is like a big neon sign, flashing in our eyes twenty-four seven. When we go to the supermarket, all we see is pregnant people or new babies. When we see our family, they ask about it and say things like, *maybe you should see a doctor* and *I warned you not to wait too long.* Andy and I fight about it as though it's one another's fault we aren't pregnant, despite the fact that we haven't been to the doctor to find out if there are any issues. We're both just tired—physically, mentally and emotionally.

The fighting started to really wear me down and when I opened up to a friend about our marriage issues, she told me about Celia Marsden's book, *Loveless Marriage.* I winced at the title when she first told me because I love Andy more than anything. It's not a loveless marriage at all. But the title is somewhat deceiving. I finished the book in two days. It was like reading about my own marriage and it made me feel relieved and hopeful.

Of course, I started following Celia on Instagram and Twitter straight away. She is an icon. Short blonde hair, always styled to per-fection, bright blue eyes and a knack for fashion. She was born to be an influencer. I have never seen her look in the slightest bit flustered or lacking in confidence. Andy reminds me that that is very much the deception of social media. We rarely see people's flaws, struggles and weaknesses, but I can just tell Celia is a boss.

We were a last minute sign up for her retreat. It took some convincing Andy but in the end he agreed we needed a break and what better than a retreat run by a couples therapist. We could find *us* again.

So, the answer is yes, I remember why I'm here.

I look at Andy and smile. 'I know. It's going to be amazing.' I lift up onto my toes and peck him on the lips.

Once we get our bags, we catch a taxi to the Sand & Salt Resort.

The driver seems to know exactly where he's going and we sit in the back seat holding hands. It almost feels like our honeymoon again. The week we spent in Thailand for our honeymoon was perfect. Certainly no mention of ovulation or prenatal vitamins.

I turn to look at Andy, a massive grin on my face. 'Are you excited?'

He returns the smile and nods. 'Definitely. I think we really need this.'

'I looked online and the pool looks incredible. And they deliver cocktails to you poolside. I know what we'll be doing this afternoon.'

Andy's smile drops. 'This isn't a party weekend, Joss. We probably shouldn't even be drinking while we're trying.'

I try not to let his comment dull my vibe. 'Babe, I'm not even ovulating and I know I'm not pregnant. What's the problem?'

'Maybe the alcohol is stopping us from getting pregnant.'

'What? The occasional glass of wine we have on the weekend? I don't think so. And I'm here to have fun with you. We paid for an all-inclusive experience, let's make the most of it.'

Andy shakes his head. Not in a way that says, *no, I won't have fun with you*. It's worse than that. It says, *I don't understand you*.

Chapter 4

Nadia

I'm beginning to regret agreeing to let Mum drive me today. We've been on the road for ten minutes, we haven't even left the Gold Coast, and she's driving me crazy. Only an hour and twenty minutes to go. *Help me.*

'Now remember, take in everything she has to say. She's an expert,' Mum says, glancing over at me for a second. I wish she'd keep her eyes on the road. 'Maybe even take notes.'

I close my eyes for a moment, trying to find a sense of calm when I want to throw myself out of the moving car and get a bus the rest of the way. I'm thirty-two years old and she has been treating me like a sad, incapable little child for months. My ex and I separated a year ago when shit hit the fan. I was okay-ish then. But when the divorce papers were finalised three months ago, I didn't handle it well.

It's not that I was upset about the marriage as such. He was a terrible person. I was disappointed that I'd failed at something. I don't fail. I never had before. Until I signed those papers.

After that, everything seemed to fail. I moved in with Mum and Dad so I could save for my own place. I lost my license drink driving one night after I'd seen a Facebook post of my ex making it official with another woman. And I was losing weight, too much weight. Not the kind of weight loss most women seem to strive for. I look ill.

From Psychologist to Influencer Sensation: Celia Marsden's Incredible Journey

A Stylish, Smart, and Multitasking Mum Takes the Digital World by Storm

By Gossip Guru Gabby
February 18th, 2019

In the world of social media, where trends change as quickly as a TikTok video, there's one influencer who's rewriting the script on success. The remarkable and incredibly intelligent Celia Marsden, a devoted mother of two, has embarked on an inspiring journey from psychologist to published author and now, an influencer who's taken the digital world by storm.

Celia Marsden's path to fame and influence is a testament to her versatility and passion for connecting with people. She first made waves in the field of psychology, where her dedication and expertise helped countless couples navigate the complexities of relationships. But Marsden had more to share, and she chose to share it with the world through her debut book, *Loveless Marriage*.

As a former psychologist, Marsden brought a unique perspective to her writing, crafting a tale that delves deep into the intricacies of modern relationships. Her book, a riveting blend of psychology and romance, resonated with readers seeking insight and understanding in matters of the heart.

The success of, *Loveless Marriage*, catapulted Marsden into the limelight, but it was her seamless transition into the world of social media that truly captured the public's imagination. Her Instagram and Twitter accounts, where she shares her thoughts on life, love and fashion quickly gained followers, who were drawn not only to her stunning style, but also to her brilliant mind.

Dressed in a manner that combines high-fashion elegance with a touch of intellectual chic, Marsden has made her mark in the influencer world as a true trendsetter. She's not just about aesthetics; she's about substance. Her online presence is marked by engaging discussions on psychology, personal development and the challenges of the modern world, all delivered with her trademark grace and authenticity.

Celia Marsden's journey from psychologist to influencer sensation is a testament to the power of personal growth and reinvention. As a multitasking mum of two, she's shown that success isn't limited to one path but can be found by following one's passion and connecting with others in meaningful ways, while managing the demands of motherhood.

So, if you're looking for inspiration in the digital age, Celia Marsden is the shining example. With her background in psychology, her literary talents and her influential presence online, she's proving that you can be both stylish, smart and a dedicated parent.

Her story is far from over, and Celia Marsden is a true trail-blazer, whose journey continues to inspire countless others to chase their dreams, embrace their own unique paths to success and to balance the joys of motherhood.

Chapter 5

Celia

The car pulls up outside the Sand & Salt Resort. It's certainly not the most luxurious place we drove past on our way along the coastline but I'm going to try and keep an open mind—something Kitty reminded me to do several times during the drive.

A woman stands outside the reception area with a smile so stiff and forced that I'm worried she'll burst into tears at any moment. Before I wrote my book, I prided myself on how approachable I was, how comfortable people were to open up to me. It was part of my job. Necessary. But since my book was published and I gained my followers, this tends to be the reaction I get from people when they're working with me, or to put it more accurately, for me. They become nervous balls of energy, threatening to explode if even the slightest thing goes wrong. At first I hated it but now I kind of enjoy the thrill.

'How long before she cracks?' I say to Kitty, turning to face her.

She shakes her head. 'You're evil. The poor woman looks petrified.'

I laugh. 'She's got no idea what she's in for.'

Lucien gets out of the car and opens my door. Kitty sighs and opens her own door to get out. Sometimes I wish she'd just relax and enjoy being treated like royalty.

My strappy wedges crunch on the gravel driveway and I wince thinking about the damage the surface will do to the soles. My Jimmy

Choos were not cut out for off-road trekking, even if it is just a few metres from the car to the building.

The woman puts out a hand to greet me. 'Hi, I'm Molly. Welcome to Sand & Salt. We're so pleased to be hosting your retreat.' She remains smiling while she speaks, which gives off a slight hint of insincerity but I'm sure it's actually just her nerves continuing to wreak havoc.

I step forward and shake her hand. It's warm and damp and I try not to let my expression show my disgust. 'Thank you for having us,' I force out.

She shakes Kitty's hand as well. Kitty gives her a warm smile and I see Molly's shoulders lower a little.

Molly has beautiful hair, I'll give her that. It's the most stunning shade of red and hangs in long waves from a neat ponytail at the back of her head. It's the kind of hair my daughter would want to play with all day long. She has smooth, pale skin, which I imagine isn't well suited to the warm weather, and her eyes are a pale sky-blue. Now that she isn't smiling maniacally at us, I can see she's quite attractive.

'Let me show you around the resort,' she says. 'Greg will get your bags.'

Right on cue, a man dressed in a navy polo and shorts walks out of the reception building. He looks to be in his fifties and like he enjoys beer far too much. I've warned my husband that if he ever lets himself go like that, I'll be out the door.

'Greg,' he puts out his hand. They really like their handshakes here. I prefer not to touch randoms but I sense Kitty's judging eyes on me so I shake his hand.

'Celia,' I say. 'And this is my friend, Kitty.'

'Great to have you, ladies,' he says in a thick Australian accent, the kind that makes me cringe. 'I'll grab your bags and get them to your rooms quick sticks.'

Molly shoots him a look.

'As soon as possible, I mean.' He corrects himself like a child scolded.

'Follow me,' Molly says in a gentle voice.

Kitty and I do as we're told and follow Molly as she takes us on a little tour of the resort. After numerous resort and villa holidays in Bali and Fiji, I'm not overly impressed. In fact, I'm a little disappointed. There's only one pool and it's smaller than our pool back at home. Spotted around the pool deck are lounges with hideous brightly coloured cushions. It looks like something out of a Target catalogue—not luxury. I've asked readers to pay good money to come here. This isn't a great start.

We get to our rooms and they're okay. The jacuzzi on the balcony with beach views makes up for the pool that looks like one at a Big 4 Caravan Park, but only Kitty and I have this luxury so my guests are still slumming it.

'Now, I've made a copy of the schedule for the weekend for all the guests and printed one for you.' Molly hands me a piece of paper with a timetable on it. I inwardly groan. Singles sessions, couples sessions, book readings, Q&A. Ugh. I probably won't even get to use the jacuzzi with all of these commitments.

'Thank you,' I say.

'I'll leave you to settle in and see you when we welcome the guests at three.'

I look down at the schedule to confirm the time, pretending to care and then I nod in agreement.

Moments after Molly closes the door, there's a knock. I open the door to see Kitty's beaming face. She rushes past me to the window and I'm still holding the schedule.

'I can't believe I've agreed to this,' I say, holding up the printed page.

Kitty barely registers that I've spoken.

I try to remind myself that I need this. *Loveless Marriage* came out years ago and the publicity had been incredible. The articles about my success as a psychologist, author and influencer were published regularly. But now, trends and popularity change as often as I change my underwear. I don't think I've featured on any websites or social media accounts in months.

I groan and place the schedule on the bench. Now Kitty turns to me from her spot overlooking the ocean.

'Ceels, how amazing is the view from the balcony.' She's practically jumping on the spot.

'Well, it ought to be considering the state of that pool area. And I don't think much of the interior design in this room.' I wave my arm behind me. 'The television is far too big for this space and who is watching television during a resort vacation? Are they hiding away from that hideous pool?'

'Celia! You're terrible. Our rooms are perfectly acceptable, more than acceptable.'

I'm about to argue when there's another knock at the door. Greg lets himself in.

'Just me, love,' he says, dragging in my suitcases. 'You sure you're just here for the weekend?'

Kitty laughs politely and I exhale loudly in response.

'Just put them by the bed, please.'

Greg wheels them over, while Kitty and I stand in silence. I'm wondering if he heard me badmouthing the place just moments ago.

Kitty's probably thinking the same thing. She'd be mortified but I think a bit of constructive criticism doesn't hurt.

'Did you ladies see the bubbles on the counter?'

I raise my eyebrows, unsure what he's talking about.

'Sorry. Molly would kill me if she heard me. The *champagne*.' He drags out the word champagne, changing the tone of his voice. 'It's Veuve. French. Meant to be pretty good.'

I stifle a snort. Personally I prefer a Dom Pérignon but Veuve will do. I'd have expected a seven dollar bottle from Dan Murphy's based on the pool cushions so it's a pleasant surprise.

'Lovely. I'll have a glass. Kitty?'

Kitty's eyes light up. She's accustomed to the seven dollar bottles, except when she comes to my place for drinks of course. 'Yes, please.'

Greg fiddles with the top of the bottle for a few minutes. 'Geez, I'm used to just cracking a can of beer. Apparently you need a licence to open these.'

I roll my eyes. 'Let me.' Exactly what kind of luxury resort is this? And Greg doesn't look like the type to be welcoming guests and pouring them champagne. He looks more like the maintenance guy.

I pop the bottle of Veuve and don't bother handing it back to Greg. I don't even want to think about the mess he'd make trying to pour it. Pouring us both a decent sized glass, I look at Kitty and smile. 'Santé,' I say.

'Cheers,' she says and clinks her glass to mine.

Greg remains by the counter. I look over at him. 'Is there something else?' I ask. Why is he just hanging around in my room while we have a drink?

'Do you need anything else?'

Kitty shakes her head.

'No, we're fine,' I say.

He nods. 'Press zero on the phone if you need anything. Someone's always in the office.' He leaves, pulling the door closed behind him.

'Well, he's nice,' Kitty says, and I swear she's almost blushing.

'You just like that he offered you a glass of decent champagne.'

She scoffs. 'They sure are trying to make a good impression on you.'

'They're not doing a very good job.'

Kitty shakes her head. 'Drink up, Celia. You're less of a snob a few wines in.'

Chapter 6
Jocelyn

A stunning redhead greets us as we pull up at the Sand & Salt Resort. Surely they shouldn't have super attractive people working at this retreat. I assume most people are here because they have relationship issues. Don't add a gorgeous woman to the equation and give our husbands a distraction. Andy has never made me feel like I need to worry but I'm human and all the reassurance in the world still makes little old me feel intimidated by beautiful women.

'I'm Molly, your host,' she says, and her voice is that annoying level of calm that people use in meditation recordings or fancy spas. 'Would you like a pomegranate mimosa while we settle you in?' A young woman next to her holds a tray of bubbly red drinks and I glance at Andy.

The drinks look delicious and so pretty but I'm very aware of Andy's sudden judginess of my drinking habits. He sighs and then reaches for two glasses.

'We'd love one, thanks,' he says, passing me a glass.

'Cheers, babe,' I say, clinking my glass to his and he smiles. He really does have model looks. I tell him all the time that his smile could melt ice shelves in Antarctica and he just rolls his eyes. We're going to be okay, I think. There's nothing I wouldn't do for Andy. If he wants me to stop drinking, I will. After this trip of course. It is our little vacation after all.

Molly gives us a printed schedule of our weekend which I find amusing. When Andy and I usually go away together, we prefer a "winging it" approach where we book flights and only a few nights' accommodation. We meet tourists and locals wherever we go and find out where we should book the next few nights of our stay, where we should eat, what activities we should do. It's how we ended up on an overnight train in Vietnam leaving us with one of our scariest and fondest memories of travelling. That's how we found out that some of the boom gates in Vietnam's countryside are manually operated and if someone isn't concentrating, a very loud bang will wake you in your four-person sleeper cabin. To have our weekend planned out with set times for meals and activities, I feel like I'm on school camp.

A man joins us in the reception area. 'G'day, guys, I'm Greg. Welcome to Sand & Salt. I'll take your bags and show you to your room. Grab a traveller if you like,' he says pointing to the tray of Mimosas.

I shake my head. 'This is enough for me for now.'

Andy and I follow a few metres behind Greg. He wheels our suitcases behind him as we pass some other rooms. He has broad shoulders, and is tanned in a way that suggests he works outside a lot. If Sand & Salt is supposed to be giving off fancy vibes, then Greg is not the guy to do it. I love an Aussie blokey bloke but we have paid for luxury.

'Pool's just there on your left. You got your cossies, yeah?'

My brow furrows momentarily at the slang.

'Yeah, bathers are packed, mate,' Andy answers for us.

The pool looks nice. Plenty of lounges so I won't have to fight for a spot or use my towel to call dibs on a place to sunbathe. Andy hates it when I get up early and put towels by the pool. Apparently, it's considered one of the most jerk moves internationally when holidaying. But I swear, everyone's doing it. The ones complaining are the ones who don't get up early enough. Where's their commitment?

Greg stops outside a room just a few metres from the pool. It's a single story, cabin-like room.

'This is yours,' he says, opening the door and letting us in before dragging our luggage in behind us.

I'm pleasantly surprised. I wouldn't call it luxury but it is beautiful. Embracing the chilled, stereotypical Byron Bay vibe, there's macramé art, rattan furniture and a stunning canvas print of the famous lighthouse. Clean and comfy, and certainly better than the Vietnamese overnight train. Although that did cost us less than the taxi ride here.

'So, are you two excited to meet Celia Marsden?' Greg asks. He's standing in the doorway to our room, leaning against the wall. This is generally the part where you would tip the bellboy and send them on their way but he doesn't look keen to move.

'Yeah,' I say. 'Super excited. I'm a huge fan of her and her book.'

Greg's smile wavers for a moment. 'I personally haven't read it. Molly has, only for research for this retreat of course. I'm more into a fishing book or a good biography.'

I smile and nod. Greg just stands there awkwardly.

'I love fishing,' Greg continues. 'We've got some great spots off the coast here. Do you guys fish?'

I steal a look at Andy who's sitting on the bed listening politely. I would very much like to be doing other things on that bed right now. But Greg doesn't take our silence as a hint to leave.

'Uh no, can't say we do.' I say.

He nods. 'Well, I should let you guys get settled. See you at the main building at three.'

I hold up the schedule. 'See you then.'

Closing the door behind him, I turn to look at Andy and burst into laughter.

'Don't be mean, Joss,' he says.

I walk over to him and he pulls me down so that I'm sitting on his knee, his arms around me.

'I'm not. But seriously, I don't recall asking for his life story. Do you reckon him and the redhead are getting it on? He knows what she's reading.' I wink.

Andy shakes his head and laughs. 'You are shocking.' He kisses my shoulder softly.

'I'm going to find out more. I'm sure there'll be a cleaner or waitress with loose lips. That's my mission, to find out the hot goss. The steamy stuff.'

Andy pushes me off his lap.

'What?' I say, feeling rejected by the move.

'Your mission this weekend is to find out goss about our resort hosts?'

My cheeks flush. I know where this is going.

'Jocelyn, what's the point of paying all that money to do this retreat if you aren't going to take it seriously.'

'I *am* taking it seriously. I'm just having a bit of fun. Relax.' I move back over to him on the bed. 'Speaking of relaxing, the schedule says we have about half an hour of free time.' I lean in to kiss him but he pulls away.

'I'm not really in the mood,' Andy says, and then goes into the bathroom.

Ouch. Rejected by my husband in the first hour of a couples retreat. Does it get any worse?

Chapter 7

Nadia

'Oh, Nadia, this looks beautiful,' Mum says, as we pull up. 'They even have people welcoming you. That's fancy.' She refers to the two women standing next to the driveway. One beautiful woman with a clipboard and another younger girl with a tray of drinks.

I roll my eyes. I don't think my parents have travelled outside Australia since they moved here from Italy, thirty-five years ago. Her experience when it comes to resorts and hotels and *fancy* is purely based on watching episode after episode of *Travel Guides*.

Mum stops the car and I get my bag out of the boot. Another car is pulling up behind us and I expect Mum to give me a quick kiss through the window and keep driving. But no, of course not. She gets out of the car and begins fussing over me.

'Have you got sunscreen packed?'

'Yes, Mum,' I groan.

A tall man steps out from the backseat of the car behind and swings a sports bag over his shoulder before saying something quickly to whoever is behind the wheel and they drive away.

The man passes us and gives a slight smile. He is incredibly handsome, with dark eyes and thick dark hair but he looks sad, almost annoyed to be here. He takes a drink from the tray and talks to the woman with the clipboard.

'Have you packed your phone charger? I don't want that thing dying. I want you to call me each day.'

'Mum, I packed everything you put on the list. You can go now.' This is so embarrassing.

'Oh wait,' Mum squeals, reaching into the backseat, and she's loud enough that the grumpy hot guy has turned around to see what's happening. 'My book. You have to get Celia to sign it. And get her to write a message. Have her write Fran, makes it sound friendly. Francesca is too formal.'

My cheeks are burning as the two retreat employees and attractive guest watch our exchange.

'Yep. Okay. Now, I love you but please leave.'

'Bye, darling,' she kisses me on both cheeks before getting in the car. Then just as she is about to drive away, she puts the window down and calls out to me. 'Don't forget to tell Celia I'm her Instagram friend and she can slide into my PMs.'

If there was an image of what mortified looked like in the dictionary, my face would be it. I close my eyes for a moment then look at her. Her face could be the dictionary image for fangirling. 'It's DMs, Mum, and yep, I'll tell her you're a fan.'

'Not in a creepy way though. You need—'

'Bye, Mum,' I cut her off.

Turning around, I'm faced with three smiles before they quickly revert back to whatever they were doing. I take a drink from the tray and am tempted to down it in one sip.

'She's sweet,' the attractive guy says. It seems my mum has lifted his mood slightly.

'Painful, actually,' I say. 'I'm Nadia.' I'm not sure if I'm saying it to him or the woman with the clipboard but they both respond.

'I'm Tanner,' he says.

'I'm Molly, your host. Welcome to Sand & Salt.' She hands Tanner and I a piece of paper each. 'This is your schedule for the weekend and Greg will show you to your rooms.'

Greg appears as if out of nowhere. 'G'day, guys,' he says, and takes my suitcase. 'Want me to take that, mate?' He gestures at Tanner's sports bag. He has certainly packed light.

'I've got it, thanks,' he says.

'Alrighty, follow me.'

Tanner and I follow as Greg leads us through the resort. I have no idea how long this walk is going to be and Greg isn't saying anything. Should I say something? It suddenly feels very awkward walking shoulder to shoulder in silence.

'I thought I was going to be the only single this weekend,' I say and immediately regret it. What if his wife is on the way? Or worse, what if he thinks I'm hitting on him? The silence was better. I'm an idiot.

'Who says I'm single?' Tanner looks at me and raises his eyebrows, and I want to walk into the hedge we're passing and hide, Homer Simpson style.

'Sorry,' I begin to say and he laughs.

'Nah, I'm divorced. Here to improve myself or whatever.'

'Me too,' I say, a little too excitedly. 'I'm so embarrassed to be divorced in my thirties. That is only meant to happen to old people, right? Like people in their—'

'Forties?' He cuts me off. Then waves as if to say, *hi, I'm the old people you're referring to.*

'No. I wasn't going to say forties. Maybe fifties though.'

He laughs.

'Anyway, I just never imagined my life like this,' I say.

'Well, here's hoping Celia can help us. And if she can't, at least you can get an autograph for your mum.'

'Stop it.' I shove him and my hand meets a rock hard bicep. I am very glad I broke the silence now. Maybe this will be more fun than I thought.

Loveless Marriage

Excerpt from the best-selling book by Celia Marsden

Seeking happiness within your relationship is not only a noble pursuit but also an essential one. Happiness is not a constant state but a dynamic and evolving experience that can be cultivated through communication, understanding and compromise. When both partners actively work towards their own happiness, while also nurturing their partner's well-being, it creates a positive synergy that strengthens the bond between them. Remember, seeking happiness together is not about perfection, but about growth and resilience. Embrace the journey, celebrate the small victories and let love be the guiding force in your pursuit of a joyful and harmonious partnership.

Equally important is the recognition that individual happiness lays the foundation for a thriving relationship. Before embarking on a shared journey, each person must invest in their own well-being, discovering what truly brings them joy, fulfilment and contentment. It's through this self-awareness and personal growth that individuals can bring their best selves into a relationship, enhancing their capacity to contribute positively to their partner's happiness. Thus, the path to a happy and enduring partnership begins with self-love and self-discovery. Only when we find happiness within ourselves can we truly share it with someone else, creating a relationship that not only survives but thrives in the face of life's challenges.

Chapter 8

Celia

I loathe meet and greets, preferring to get my message across on Instagram or Twitter, or more recently trying my hand at TikTok. It doesn't even matter what I post, the likes, comments and shares go through the roof and each one gives me a little buzz. But sharing what I do in person, face-to-face, it doesn't have the same effect. Is the nod of a head the equivalent of a "like" or is applause equal to a "share"? How do I know if the meet and greet is a success without the analytics to tell me?

This will be the first time my guests meet me and I need to make a good first impression. It's a strange feeling to want to impress people who are below you, who are here to improve themselves or their relationships. They should be wanting to impress me. And yet, here I am touching up my make up for the third time.

'Ceels!' Kitty calls, from the other side of the front door. 'We're going to be late.'

I open the door and she enters in a stunning green kaftan that shows off her long, athletic legs. I inwardly groan. I wish I had the genetics that allowed me to eat what I want and wear what I want.

'You look great, Kitty Kat.'

She beams. 'Thanks. I got this for a steal off Marketplace. I could never afford Camilla otherwise.'

I smile. Camilla had approached me several times to work together on a promotion but my manager, Megan, said it just wasn't "on-brand" enough. 'Are you going swimming?'

'Not today. Can't miss your welcome meeting. Moral support and whatever.' She shrugs.

'Thank you, but I warn you, it's going to be boring and you'll have to mingle with the commoners.'

'Celia!' she shouts. 'I'm a *commoner*, too, remember? And these people paid a lot of money to be here.'

I flick my hand at her. *Whatever*, I think to myself. Kitty always gets funny when I discuss money and status. I assume it's the jealousy thing. But also, sometimes she's just downright bitchy. We'll see how she performs as my best friend this weekend.

A recreation lounge next to the reception building was listed on the itinerary as the space to be used for the welcome meeting and where I will be conducting the one-on-one and couples therapy sessions over the coming days. Kitty and I are the first to arrive, besides Molly, who is busying herself setting up some chairs.

'Oh, Ms Marsden, I'm so sorry. Just finishing the set up. What a hectic day.'

Molly looks frazzled. Her cheeks are pink and a layer of sweat shines on her face.

'Let us help you with these chairs,' Kitty says, as she drags two chairs from against the wall to join a row already started by Molly.

There's no way I'm helping set this up. I'm the guest of honour. I'm making this place a lot of money. I am not here as an extra set of hands for their laborious tasks.

Kitty looks at me, her eyes burning into mine, trying—and failing—to convince me to help.

'Oh please, don't. Just leave those.' Molly motions at Kitty and the chairs she's holding. 'I'm just about done.'

There are about thirty chairs facing a makeshift lectern when Molly smooths her hands down her black skirt and sighs. 'Okay, we're ready. Can I get you anything before the others arrive?'

'A bottle of water would be lovely. Preferably sparkling.'

'Of course.' She nods and scurries away.

Glancing around the room, I'm immediately disappointed with the lighting. There are only two windows letting in a small amount of afternoon light. There are a handful of downlights and three big bulbs that hang down over a pool table. The table is currently covered and out of use for this weekend, along with the other items in this room, including table tennis and foosball. I imagine this is where the kids would have a blast on family holidays. This weekend, it's my workspace. *Gross.*

'Kitty, can you run back to the room and get my ring light?'

She rolls her eyes. 'Be right back.'

I've asked Kitty to photograph me during my meet and greet and at other stages throughout the weekend. Megan thinks it'll look great for my profile if others see the work I'm doing. However, I don't care what kind of "photoshoot" it is, I need decent lighting.

I step up to the lectern, which is actually just a tall bar table with a portable microphone on it and I lay out some notes that I jotted down on the plane earlier. I also set up a copy of my book at the front of the tall table. These guests will likely already know my book but it never hurts to have it in all of the photos Kitty takes or the ones these guests snap from their phones to share on social media.

Kitty rushes in with my ring light, which she sets up a metre away from the table and I instruct her on the best angles for ensuring the light isn't seen but still highlights my face.

'Maybe you should have brought Megan on this trip,' she says, after I show her how to apply a filter before photographing. 'I'm not cut out for this.'

'You have to pay for your trip somehow, Kitty Kat.'

She scowls but before she can say anything, the first guest arrives.

A shy-looking brunette enters the room with her arms wrapped tightly around a book that she hugs to her chest. She looks up for a moment and makes eye contact with me, smiling briefly before looking back down at her feet.

She edges her way to a seat near the front and pauses before sitting down. She takes a deep breath and then blurts out, 'Hi. Um, I'm Nadia. I'm super sorry but can you sign this for my mum. She's a huge fan. Her name is Francesca, but can you write "To Fran", please. I mean, that's if you're signing books. I know that's not why you're here. But, yeah, I said I'd ask and she'd kill me if I didn't.'

Before she can continue her nonsense speech, I take the book from her hands and smile.

'That's fine. Fran, you said?'

Nadia nods.

'Kitty, make sure you're getting this?'

Kitty gets the camera ready and moves around capturing different angles of me signing the book.

I pass the book back to Nadia.

'Thank you so much,' she beams. 'Mum is going to be ecstatic when she sees this.'

'Great,' I say. 'Just take a seat.' Then I whisper to Kitty. 'See, I'm approachable. Megan says I can be a bit stand-offish but that was very friendly, if I do say so myself.'

'Well, at least someone's saying so.'

I flash her a wicked grin.

Several more guests, plus Molly, trickle in—some in pairs and others alone. I stand behind the lectern, nodding as they enter but not moving. They all watch me like I'm the new animal at the zoo, waiting for me to do something exciting—swing from a tree, roar from a high-up rock or chomp leaves from tall trees. But I only resemble one animal from the zoo. The leopard—calm, ready to pounce and I look great in a print.

When the seats are full, Molly stands next to me at the tall table.

'Welcome to Sand & Salt. We are so excited to be hosting you all for this special event with the wonderful, Celia Marsden.'

The guests clap. I smile. Kitty snaps photos of myself and the audience.

'I trust you have all settled into your rooms. Please, don't hesitate to reach out to Greg, myself or any other staff member if there is something we can do to make your stay more enjoyable.' She takes a deep breath and clasps her hands together. 'So, without further ado, please welcome, Celia Marsden.'

There is more clapping, a few wolf whistles and some guests hold their phones up in front of them, presumably taking photos. I put my shoulders back and lift my chin, ensuring the angle they catch is fit for social media.

I clear my throat. 'Thank you, Molly, and everyone here at Sand & Salt for having me. This is the first retreat I've hosted and I'm honoured to be working with a group of couples and singles who are here because they need to make a change in their lives.'

People in the audience nod.

'I'm proud to say that I have changed so many lives through my book, *Loveless Marriage*. I've helped couples rebuild their relationship when all seemed lost and I've given people the courage to leave their spouses when they realised their relationship was beyond repair, that they deserved happiness in solitude.'

There's a sharp inhale from somewhere in the room and one man in the second row coughs loudly into his hand. It's not something I had intended to happen when I wrote my book. I did write about the fact that divorce is sometimes the best option for some couples but ultimately my goal has always been to help couples improve their relationship. In saying that, I am a big believer in being in a relationship for the right reasons and I guess that came through in my writing and gave people some perspective. Some people this weekend could be in for a shock.

'This weekend I will work with the couples in a traditional style couples therapy session, allowing you both to be heard, and I'll work with the newly single people as you navigate this change in your life.'

I'd been nervous when Megan suggested we open this retreat up to singles too. I'm a *couples* counsellor after all. Sure, I've done plenty of sessions with people on their own in the early days or when a spouse doesn't show up to an appointment but I haven't done a heap of *let me help you find you* type sessions. But there's enough rubbish sprinkled on websites and social media for me to borrow from. Meditate, exercise, keep a diary, practise gratitude. Blah, blah, blah. I can do this.

'In order for us to all feel comfortable this weekend, I want everyone to introduce yourself with your name and where you're from. No need for details about why you're here but feel free to share anything else you like with the group. Then we'll have some free time before our first dinner tonight.'

I hate ice-breaker activities. *Hate, hate, hate them.* But I have a short amount of time with these people and I need them to feel comfortable from the get-go. The friendlier they are with the other guests, the more comfortable they'll feel with me. *I hope.*

'You did great, Ceels,' Kitty says. She pours us a glass of champagne as we take a seat on my balcony after the meet and greet.

'Thanks. Sorry you had to witness the boring introductions.'

'Nah, I liked it. I have a lot of downtime this weekend; I need people to talk to.'

I look at her and draw my eyebrows together. 'Really? You're going to befriend them?' I couldn't think of anything worse.

'I'll be friendly of course. I'm not saying we'll leave with each other's number or Instagram handle but I'm not going to sit in stilted silence all day.'

I just shake my head. 'Right. So, who've you got your eye on to replace me as your bestie?' I tease.

'Oh, I don't know. Nadia seemed sweet but a little shy and intense. The Lambert couple reminded me of your parents, Ceels. So cute in their matching outfits. But like them, most of the couples look a fair bit older.'

I picture the Lamberts coming up to meet me after the introductions—very formal and proper. I guess that is kind of like my parents. He was average height, grey hair and bordering on overweight, while she was petite, which was very at odds with her oversized gold-chain necklace.

'Jocelyn and Andy didn't look old,' I say, picturing instead the handsome man and his young wife.

'Hard to see Jocelyn's face when she held her phone in front of it the whole time, recording you.'

I laugh. 'Yes, she seemed a little obsessed.' I flick my hair. 'Can you blame her?'

Kitty almost spits out her wine. 'Lachy did too. He barely blinked as he soaked up your every word.'

'Yes, but he was creepy. He didn't smile. The only time he showed any kind of emotion was when he had a coughing fit while I talked about my book.'

'His gift was super sweet,' Kitty says.

'An engraved pen? It's weird.'

She shrugs. 'You're going to have your hands full this weekend. There are some interesting characters for you to "fix" or whatever it is you do. Anyway, have you heard from Tom?'

Tom is my husband of ten years. When we met he was an accountant and now he's a stay-at-home dad and my personal assistant, photographer, taxi driver, etc. I think he was pretty happy to quit his job to stay home with our children, Jack and Ava, but with Jack at school now and Ava in kinder, I can tell he's getting bored. I don't think he wants to chase me around and take photos of me for the rest of his life. It sucks because I've trained him well and I like not having to cook or clean anymore. He's the perfect house-husband. And the perfect arm-candy for events, often mistaken for Chris Evans—not the clean shaven Captain America version, but the sexy beard version. Not that he knows it. He will still happily go out in tracksuit pants, a stained shirt and crocs. *Ummm, you're married to Celia Marsden. That is entirely unacceptable.*

At least I've managed to educate him on dressing the children. I have partnerships with a number of online boutique brands that do adorable kids clothing. My kids don't need to wear the same K-Mart jumper that every other child at the playground is wearing.

'Yes,' I say. 'I sent him a text when we arrived earlier, and he said the kids went off to school and kindergarten just fine.'

'I miss the kids so much already,' Kitty says.

She has two kids, as well, who are similar ages to Ava and Jack.

'Mmm, me too,' I lie.

I'm a little ashamed to admit it but I don't miss the kids. I always wanted children and of course I love them, but they're not on my mind twenty-four-seven. I don't know if that makes me a cold-hearted bitch. I'd never say it out loud. I love taking Ava to Disney On Ice or the theatre. She loved the stage show of Julia Donaldson's, *The Gruffalo*. Jack prefers coming with me to the tennis or sitting in a box at the Big Bash matches. I leave the everyday activities, the mess, the complaining to Tom.

I take a big sip of champagne. 'I'm going to go get ready for dinner,' I say, before leaving Kitty on the balcony to go inside.

Chapter 9

Jocelyn

'Oh my gosh, Andy, look at this one!' I thrust my phone in front of Andy. There's a photo of Celia and I from the welcome meeting. She'd looked so classy in a white collared shirt and tailored forest-green shorts. Meanwhile, I'd been sweating, my legs sticking to the chair and the humidity already causing my hair to become a frizzy, golden nest. Still, the photo was nice.

Andy looks over at my phone and nods, clearly uninterested. I open Instagram and flick through the filters, hoping to look slightly more decent when standing next to *the* Celia Marsden.

'Are you really going to post that on social media?'

'Yeah, obviously,' I say. Surely my husband knows me better than that. I unashamedly live my life through my social media pages. I mean, I only have a handful of followers, all of which are family and friends, but yes, I will be posting it.

'But everyone will know we're on a couples retreat. Won't they ask questions?'

'There's no shame in wanting to improve our marriage, babe. Plus, it's such a great location anyway. Who wouldn't want a weekend away in Byron?'

Andy shrugs.

It'll be fine, I remind myself. There's nothing wrong with our relationship. We're just in a rut because we've had no success falling pregnant. It must happen to lots of couples.

I upload the photo. *The people you meet on vacay @celiamarsden #goals.*

Then I slide off my dress and get comfy on the lounge by the pool. Andy is next to me, his strong chest glowing in the hot, Australian sun. His skin doesn't burn the way mine does and I'm so envious.

'Honey, can you put cream on my back?' I ask, and he sits himself up, his abs flexing with the movement. It certainly wasn't a lack of attraction getting in the way of us having a baby. 'Wait, before your hands get all slimy, let's take a selfie.'

Andy rolls his eyes but complies. Then he rubs the SPF50 into my back, carefully covering every inch. He's learnt how easily I burn and didn't take well to rubbing aloe vera into a peeling canvas the last time I got burnt.

'Done,' he says, before lying down again. I lie next to him and he takes my hand. 'We should talk about what we want to get out of these sessions with Celia.'

My body stiffens. 'Ummm. I actually don't know.'

Andy sighs. I know he hates my answer. It's the answer I always give. I don't know what to say. I love Andy, I want Andy but there's something missing...well, for him anyway.

'We've been trying to have a baby for a while now,' Andy says. 'And you're getting frustrated tracking everything and I'm feeling hopeless and it's taking a toll. Sex is...is a chore now.'

'Not for me,' I say, defensively. I'm happy to do it whenever he wants, I'd just rather not pee on a stick beforehand to ensure I'm ovulating. That's not my kind of foreplay.

He squeezes my hand. 'You know what I mean, Jossy. We're just so uptight lately.'

'I think we should stop trying,' I blurt out. I hadn't been planning to say it. I'd definitely been thinking it for a while now. But I didn't know it was sitting there, ready to escape my lips before I had a chance to really think about the consequences.

'What?' he asks, yanking his hand from mine and propping himself up on his elbow to face me.

'Like not permanently. Just have a break. Enjoy each other again. Let's relax.'

'How long have you been thinking this? Why did we just pay all that money for a couples retreat if you want to ignore the issue, not fix it? Is it just because you wanted a photo for your Instagram page?'

His words sting. I sit up, swinging my feet around to find my sandals on the ground. 'This is what I mean. You're so snappy lately. I'm going to get a cocktail. You want one?'

He shakes his head before turning onto his stomach, facing away from me.

There is poolside service but I go to the bar at one end of the pool area, I just want to get away from Andy for a moment. Sometimes I don't think he realises the toll it all takes on me. He just has to show up and *plant the seed*. I'm the one using tracking apps, peeing on sticks, eating the right foods, peeing on more sticks and then breaking the inevitable bad news to him. It's a physical and emotional load that I need a break from.

There are a few other people around the pool on lounges and some sitting around the bar too. A woman who introduced herself as Nadia is at the bar. She is stunningly beautiful, like a Victoria's Secret runway model, but in a way where she doesn't know it because her shoulders are hunched and her long dark hair hides much of her beautiful face. She's talking to Tanner.

Nadia and Tanner had both introduced themselves as being single so I suppose it makes sense that the singles would mingle. Who would they talk to all weekend otherwise? But the way Tanner's body is positioned on the bar stool, one knee against the bar and the other against Nadia's stool, almost like he's holding it there in place, makes me think Tanner likes what he sees. And obviously. She's gorgeous. But Celia did make a point of the fact that the singles are here to find themselves, to better themselves. Not to find love.

'This isn't *Love Island*,' Celia had said with a grin at the welcome meeting.

'I wish,' I'd whispered to Andy when she'd said it. The scandal and shenanigans that went down on that show were bloody delicious.

I order myself a cocktail and then decide to get Andy a beer. A peace offering. While the bartender shakes my cosmopolitan, I watch Nadia and Tanner. She tucks her hair behind her ear and straightens her back, seeming to slowly relax into whatever conversation her and Tanner are having. I wish I could hear them. He leans in and whispers something to her and she giggles softly, her eyelids fluttering. *Oh, these two are doomed.*

I take my cocktail and Andy's beer back over to our lounges.

'Babe, got you a beer.'

He rolls over onto his back. 'I said I didn't want anything.'

'Call it an olive branch. A reset button. Let's have a nice time this weekend.'

He sighs and takes the bottle from my hand. 'Cheers, Joss.'

I smile. 'So, guess what I just saw?'

'A Hemsworth?'

I playfully punch his hard bicep. 'No. Those singles. Nadia and Tanner. They're flirting at the bar. My bet is they'll bang before the weekend's over.' I bounce up and down on the spot with excitement. 'Ohhh, I hope it happens.'

'Really? That's what you're hoping for.'

Here we go again. Oh man, I'm over these constant arguments.

He continues, 'I thought this beer was a peace offering. A toast to us having a good weekend. Not a drink to share while you fill me in on meaningless gossip. For once, can you focus on us?'

I blink back tears. Shocked at the outburst. Since we've been here our marriage is getting worse by the minute. I take my sunglasses from the top of my head and press them firmly onto my face, hoping to hide any sign of how much that hurt.

'Sure,' I whisper. And we lie there in silence.

Chapter 10

Molly

'I think that went well. Do you think that went well?' I ask Greg.

My mind is in overdrive—replaying every moment of each guest's arrival, of Celia's welcome meeting, of the first "free-time" block of the weekend. Did the guests have drinks when they wanted them? Were there enough pool lounges? Was the pool warm enough? Most importantly, was Celia happy with how she was spending her free time? After all, it was her opinion, and her followers, that were the priority.

Greg places his hands on my shoulders. 'You've gotta relax, Mol. You'll give yourself a heart attack before the woman even has a chance to twit, or whatever it is you're hoping for.'

I look him in the eye. His heavy hands calm me, but only slightly. 'It's tweet,' I say. 'And it's hard to relax when there's so much depending on this weekend.' Visions of me rocking up on Mum and Dad's doorstep with a suitcase and no life plan haunt my mind's eye.

'Mate, everything is going to plan. Nothing to worry about.'

I wish I believed him. I also wish I had just a fraction of his ability to stay calm. I swear Sand & Salt could be in the pathway of a tropical cyclone and Greg's heart rate wouldn't even change. Meanwhile, my Apple watch keeps flashing my increasing stress level at me and prompting me to use a breathing app. There's no time for breathing apps this weekend.

'By the way,' Greg adds, 'one of the guests was asking about security. Apparently worried about theft.'

My eyebrows furrow at the idea of it at the resort. I can't recall there ever being an incident of theft. We have cameras around reception but that's so I can keep an eye on the desk if I'm doing other jobs around the place. There aren't cameras outside the rooms and certainly not inside.

'Just remind them there are safes in each room.'

'Righto,' Greg says, and he heads out of the dining room where I'm left to do the final preparations before dinner service.

I put a menu on each of the tables. It's a set menu, with some room to cater for dietary requirements. Usually, we run the space like a restaurant with a small selection of options but Carlos was keen to do a set menu, make it fancy. Although, I suspect he was also a little nervous about all the guests eating at the same time rather than the sporadic dining that normally happens. Either way, I was happy with this option because I didn't need to take orders—there could be no mistakes or miscommunication between Carlos and me.

I read through the final menu before I place it down.

Appetiser: Caramelised Chilli Prawns.

Shit.

I march over to the kitchen, waving the menu in front of me.

'Carlos!' I shout.

The short, stocky man pops his head out from the walk-in refrigerator. 'Molly,' he says, in his thick Italian accent.

'What is this?' I say, pointing at the menu.

He flinches at my tone and a ripple of guilt flows through my body. But no, I've got to stay strong. This is important.

He shrugs.

'Seafood,' I say. 'Your appetiser is seafood. Celia says she doesn't eat seafood.'

'No, no. You said, the *smell* of fish makes her sick.'

'Right. So why are you serving her this?'

'Well, my prawns don't smell.'

He says it so matter-of-factly, so honestly, that it makes me even more annoyed. I take a deep breath. It's too late to change the menu and recreate more than twenty new appetisers.

'Perhaps you could just make something different for Celia? Just in case.'

Carlos' shoulders slump and his dark, bushy eyebrows sink low over his eyes. 'Of course, Molly,' he says, in a tone that makes my guilt multiply tenfold. 'I will prepare a mushroom risotto for her. My specialty.'

My heart rate begins to lower. 'Thank you, Carlos. Sounds wonderful.'

I scurry back out to the dining area and brief Lisa on the change. She's a local, working part-time while she studies. She's only nineteen but she's a hard worker and her enthusiasm is definitely higher than usual with an influencer amongst us.

'Looks great in here,' Lisa says, as we wait for the guests.

I think she's trying to fill the awkward silence, while we stand there. Usually this would never happen. Guests would file in and out of the dining room all day for breakfast, lunch, late lunch, early dinners—there was always someone in here ready to take orders. We've never had an empty dining room awaiting a scheduled dinner.

'Thanks,' I say. 'Now, remember, let me handle Celia's table and you focus on our other guests.'

She nods, just as the door to the dining room swings open.

The prawn dish looks like a work of art. The presentation, the colours, the aroma wafting into the air—all incredible. Carlos was right. His prawns don't smell. I hope he's kept some extras aside for Lisa and me to pick at later.

The guests seat themselves wherever they like and for the most part the couples are sitting in groups and the singles are in groups. Kitty and Celia are at a table with two couples. One of them, the young couple with the overexcited female and insanely handsome guy, Andy—couldn't forget his name. The other couple are much older, the Lamberts. They'd spent the afternoon playing a quick nine holes at a local golf course. Greg had shuttled them there and back.

'Caramelised chilli prawns,' I say. I place a plate down in front of Kitty and her eyes light up.

'Thank you,' she says.

Then I place a bowl in front of Celia. While Carlos' mushroom risotto is one of my personal favourites from our regular menu, it is certainly not as appealing to the eye. Multiple shades of brown slopped into a little mound, sprinkled with some parmesan.

'And the non-seafood alternative tonight is mushroom risotto. Bon appétit.'

Lisa places the remaining prawn dishes in front of the others seated with Celia. Celia looks around at the other plates. Her eyes narrow and my breath catches.

She looks up at me. Her blonde bob is dead straight, not a hair out of place and her blue eyes are cold. 'Um, what is this?' Celia looks down at the risotto.

'You mentioned you didn't like seafood so our chef prepared you something else.'

Celia huffs, shaking her head. 'No. I believe I said I don't like the *smell* of seafood. I eat seafood.'

Then why the hell mention it? I think to myself. If I send you an email asking for dietary requirements and you say you don't like the smell of fish, I assume that means it's not in your diet. The question was not, "Which odours do you dislike?", to which I would currently answer with the scent of Celia's ghastly, strong, expensive perfume that she has over-sprayed.

But I smile. 'I'm so sorry. Must've been a misunderstanding.' I pick up Celia's bowl. 'I'll have the chef prepare you the prawns right now.'

The inevitable *told you so* face from Carlos is painful but Celia is delighted with her prawns so I bury my pride.

Only two more courses to go.

Chapter 11

Nadia

Dinner is a welcome lining to my stomach. Although, probably a little late. I lost track of time and how many cocktails I had with Tanner at the pool bar.

He sits next to me at a table in the restaurant, along with two single women in their fifties and a single guy who's forty. We'd already met during our icebreaker earlier but we reintroduce ourselves anyway.

It doesn't get past me that I am the youngest. Being divorced so young is one of the harshest realities of my situation. Mum reminds me that it's a positive that this happened before I got older, before kids were involved. "You still have so many reproductive years ahead of you," she says. And whilst I know she's trying to make me feel better, any mention of reproducing has my chest tightening because I'm thirty-two. I already feel the clock ticking. Not to mention the fact that I'd been ready to start trying for children with my ex. We'd spoken about it and he always had a reason to wait a little longer. I'd probably still be waiting if I hadn't tried to surprise him at the office one evening and found him screwing his assistant. Said assistant is now six months pregnant with his child. Go figure.

I try to remember why I'm here. I'm here to find the old Nadia, to find happiness within myself again. And you're never too young or too old to find what makes you happy.

I steal a glance at Tanner while we eat our appetisers. Lachy, the forty year old single, has been speaking non-stop for five minutes about his divorce. I know every detail of the texts he sent his ex-wife, begging her to take him back. He's really trying to sell himself as a romantic but hasn't explained *why* she kicked him out yet. There's always two sides to every story.

Tanner gives me a knowing smile. I bet he's thinking the same thing. We had so much in common when we were talking earlier. Just surface stuff like we're both Queenslanders, who enjoy the outdoors and the beach. We both follow an AFL team despite living in the heart of NRL territory. And, obviously, we're both recently divorced. Although the conversation hasn't turned that direction yet.

And I don't know if it will. It certainly won't while Lachy has the floor.

'So then,' Lachy says. 'I wrote her notes. I left them on her windscreen or at her office.'

One of the women at the table interrupts him. 'That's actually a little creepy, don't you think?'

Lachy smiles at her. His blonde moustache quirks up as he does so. 'Creepy or romantic?'

The woman visibly grits her teeth but says nothing.

A young waitress interrupts—*thank you!*—and serves us our main meal. I'm too hungry to listen to her explanation but whatever this meat is, it's cooked to perfection. I try to remember to look elegant as I inhale my meal but it's hard when you're a little tipsy and the food is this good. Besides, who's watching?

'Hungry?' Tanner whispers, and I turn to see him grinning at me. And such a devilish grin.

My cheeks redden. Ugh. This is so embarrassing.

I use my napkin to pat at some gravy on my lip. 'I'm Italian. I'm always hungry.' A lie since this is probably the most I've eaten at a meal in months but it makes him laugh so mission accomplished.

After dinner, Molly introduces Carlos to us all.

'If you have any requests or questions, please speak to myself or Carlos. We want to ensure your stay is perfect.'

Carlos stands next to her smiling and when he speaks, my body feels warm with familiarity at his accent. 'Your dessert today will be a *Roman* dessert. I will be *roaming* the room with various small treats.' He chuckles at his joke and a few people give him a sympathetic sound or exhale that indicates a laugh. 'This way you can get to know each other. Have fun.' Then he hurries off to the kitchen, saying nothing else.

'Do you really want to get to know anyone else?' Tanner leans over to say. 'I've kind of had enough of introductions after Lachy.'

I nod. 'Yeah. He is intense.'

'Want to go for a walk?'

'And miss dessert?' Not really. If the first two courses were that good, imagine how dessert will be. But I only hesitate for a second because then he leans back, stretching his arms and his shirt rises up enough for me to see the skin just above his waistband. And it looks better than any dessert I've had. 'Sure. Let's go.'

The sun is slowly setting behind the mountains in the distance, while the ocean before us reflects the sunset's pinks and golds. Tanner and I walk to a grassy spot above the sand and sit down. We took a bottle of wine and some glasses on our way out. No one seemed to notice or if they did, they didn't care.

My stomach is fluttering. I haven't felt much of anything, let alone excitement, in a long time. I don't even know why I feel like this. He's just another divorcee getting some help and I literally met him like six hours ago. But in six hours, he has made me smile and laugh more than I have in the last six months. That must mean something. Not to mention, the other feelings he stirs. The deeper ones. The ones I thought must've died along with my marriage because I have not given a man a second glance since my ex.

But Tanner is something else. Sure, he's traditionally handsome—tall, dark hair and by the pool bar earlier, I spied some very toned abs and arms. But it's not just that. His eyes are mesmerising, as though they've seen the world. It's like all of his emotions spill from there and when I look into them, I feel lost. I want to ask him every single thing he's thinking or feeling in that moment.

Right now, his eyes sparkle in the last rays of sunlight and he smiles. 'So,' he says, 'what do you think of the retreat so far?'

I shrug. 'I suppose it's really just been like a holiday. We don't start the real stuff until tomorrow.'

To be honest, I am dreading the *real* stuff—the sessions with Celia. The deep stuff. The feelings stuff. What am I supposed to say? Mum said I just need to be honest. But how embarrassing to tell someone that I was cheated on and then went off the rails because he changed his relationship status. Who am I? Some sort of *Geordie Shore* crazy girl. I should've been better than that, stronger.

'I'm not looking forward to that,' Tanner says, and I'm relieved that he feels the same way. 'But I guess that's why I'm here. To put it all out there.'

I nod but don't look at him, instead fiddling with the strap on my sandal.

'Are you okay?' he asks.

I look up at him and his eyes are now darker with concern, the twinkle faded. 'Mmm, just same as you. Not looking forward to it. I'm embarrassed.'

'I'm sure you have nothing to be embarrassed about.' He scoots closer to me so that our thighs are almost touching. I can feel the warmth of his body, which is a welcome relief now that the sun is down and the breeze off the ocean is chilly. 'How about I tell you why I'm here and then you can tell me why you're here.'

My chest tightens. *Absolutely not.* But then he leans back on his hands, his big, strong body turning to me and I'm safe. A feeling I haven't had in so long. Maybe I need to own it and get on with my life.

I sigh. 'Okay, let's do it.'

We drop the empty glasses and bottle at the dining room, which is now dark. Tanner walks me back to my room and I can't believe how different I feel now. It's as though he lifted a ten ton truck off my shoulders and made it disappear.

He didn't judge me. He wasn't disgusted. He just listened.

When we get to my door, I turn to him. 'Thank you,' I say, and I wish I could say more but there is just far too much mush going around in my brain right now.

He had told me about his ex-wife and how it was her that recommended he did the retreat. My ex blocked my number and all my social media accounts when we split up. The relationship Tanner still has with his ex is foreign to me, and stirs a small feeling of jealousy within.

'No, thank you. It was good to talk about it. As you now know, I don't have a heap of people in my life to talk to these days.'

I nod and give him a reassuring smile. Tanner had been married to his job, in a senior position as a detective, and rarely at home. Apparently when he was at home, he was still working. His wife had had enough and he'd understood but had been heartbroken, nonetheless. He turned to alcohol—another thing we have in common—became depressed and angry, pushed away his friends and ended up being demoted after a few personal issues followed him to work. I feel like our stories are aligned in so many ways. Except for the fact that Tanner's ex read *Loveless Marriage* and convinced him to come here to meet Celia and get help. Whereas, mine would quite happily see me drop off the face of the Earth.

'I'm glad you told me,' I say.

He steps closer to me and my breath hitches. I hope he didn't notice.

'Me too.' He reaches out and tucks a strand of loose hair behind my ear. My skin tingles where his hand grazes my cheek. 'Seems like we both need a little help adjusting to our new lives.'

I could get used to my new life if this guy was standing in front of me in it.

This is so crazy. I met him today.

His hand lingers for an extra moment and we stand in silence, staring at each other. The tension is palpable and I have to remind myself to breathe. I run my tongue over my lip and he leans closer.

'Hey, guys,' a voice calls from a few room's down. Tanner drops his hand and we jump apart, looking like two teenagers being sprung making out behind the school lockers.

It's Greg. What's he doing outside our rooms this late? I check my watch. Midnight. *Shit.* We're meant to do sunrise yoga tomorrow morning to "prepare our bodies and minds for change". The only thing my body will be prepared for is strong coffee.

He approaches us and his smile drops. 'I thought you two were part of the singles group.'

It really is like school. Only I'm thirty-two and my teacher is some bogan bloke with a pot belly.

Tanner speaks up. He doesn't sound startled or embarrassed, the way I feel right now. 'We are. We were just sharing divorce stories.'

Greg's eyes widen and Tanner laughs. It lightens the mood.

'Don't worry,' Tanner says. 'Divorce isn't a dirty word.'

Greg clears his throat. 'No.' More throat clearing. 'Of course not. Look, I'm just out here because one of the other guests heard some strange noises before. Did you see anything?'

I look at Tanner and then back at Greg, shaking my head. 'No. We've been at the beach,' I say, and I immediately regret it. *Are we allowed to go to the beach whenever we want? Oh my gosh, stop. You're an adult. You paid to be here. You can do what you like.*

Greg nods. 'Okay, no worries.' He starts down the path in the direction of reception before he stops. 'Hey. Just be careful wandering around so late, yeah?'

'Sure,' Tanner says. Then he turns to me. 'That was weird.'

'Yeah,' I say, letting out a small huff of a laugh.

I desperately want to be back where we were a few minutes ago but the moment has passed.

I swipe the key card to open my door. 'Thanks again,' I say. 'See you tomorrow.'

Tanner smiles. 'Looking forward to it.'

I shut the door behind me and then lean back against it, close my eyes and sigh. My heart is racing and I want to fall asleep right now so that the morning comes quicker and I can talk to him again.

But when I open my eyes, my stomach drops.

The air around me feels thicker somehow.

Someone has been in my room. Or are they still here?

I should just leave. Go and get Tanner. Or Greg. Or call the cops. I don't know.

But I don't. Call it the wine, maybe the conversation or the not-quite-enough touching but whatever it is, I don't get help. I move towards my suitcase, which is now open. I know for a fact I closed it because I hid my laptop in there. We weren't supposed to bring computers but I like to fall asleep watching rom-coms on it. Some kind of cruel ritual I put myself through.

I lift up the clothing on top, the laptop is still there. *Weird*. That's the only valuable thing in there. What's the point?

Then it catches my eye. A note on my bedside table above the suitcase. Resort stationery and block handwriting.

You're not here to meet someone. Do the right thing. -CM

Loveless Marriage: Controversial Book by Celia Marsden Sparks Divorce Debate

By Arrow Winters
23rd September, 2018

In the world of relationship advice literature, few books have ignited as much controversy and passionate debate as *Loveless Marriage*, penned by renowned couples therapist, Celia Marsden. Published last year, this groundbreaking work has garnered both accolades and criticism for its bold message encouraging couples to consider divorce as a valid option for finding happiness and personal fulfilment.

Celia Marsden, a seasoned expert in couples therapy, has built her career on helping people navigate the tumultuous waters of relationships. In *Loveless Marriage*, she presents a compelling argument that staying in an unhappy and unfulfilling marriage can sometimes do more harm than good. Drawing from her extensive experience working with couples on the brink of separation, Marsden challenges conventional wisdom by asserting that divorce, when approached thoughtfully and responsibly, can be a pathway to a more fulfilling life.

The book's premise, however, has sparked a wave of anger and criticism from traditionalists who believe that it undermines the sanctity of marriage. Critics argue that Marsden's work promotes the idea of "throwaway relationships" and could potentially contribute to the breakdown of families. Some conservative voices have even accused her of profiting from the pain and suffering of couples.

Conversely, Marsden has garnered significant support from those who believe her book empowers individuals to make informed choices about their relationships. Supporters argue that *Loveless Marriage* provides a much-needed voice for people trapped in unhappy unions, offering them guidance and validation as they contemplate divorce. Marsden's work has been praised for challenging societal norms that often pressure individuals to stay in toxic relationships at the expense of their own well-being.

Marsden herself remains steadfast in her conviction that *Loveless Marriage* is a necessary contribution to the dialogue on relationships. She contends that her book encourages individuals to take responsibility for their own happiness and well-being, ultimately leading to healthier, more fulfilling lives. In response to critics, she emphasises that her intent is not to promote divorce indiscriminately but to empower individuals to make choices that align with their values and long-term happiness.

While *Loveless Marriage* has undoubtedly ignited controversy, it has also sparked essential conversations about the nature of marriage, individual happiness and the role of therapists in guiding couples through difficult decisions. Whether one views the book as a groundbreaking catalyst for personal growth or a dangerous assault on the institution of marriage, there's no denying that Celia Marsden's work has left an indelible mark on the world of relationship literature, challenging us all to rethink the ways we approach love, commitment and personal fulfilment.

Chapter 12

Celia

S urprisingly, I sleep well, despite the feeling of dread about today. I start the therapy sessions later this morning and already some of the guests are painful from just my interactions with them at dinner. The way some of them speak to one another, their behaviour, their complete lack of effort when it comes to appearance—if you don't respect yourself, how can you expect someone else to respect you? And don't get me started on the singles. All woe is me, I'm such a victim. Highly unattractive.

There's a knock on my door at five to six. Who is bothering me at this hour? I wrap a robe around myself and open the door. Kitty greets me, her long, slender body covered in tight activewear.

She frowns when she sees me. 'Aren't you coming to sunrise yoga?'

Is she serious? There's absolutely no way I'm going to willingly join in on an optional activity with guests. I don't want to bend my body this way and that around *them*. And I certainly don't want to see them doing it.

'Uh, hard pass.'

Kitty rolls her eyes. 'Come on. It'll be good to stretch after yesterday's travel day and it's nice out already.'

I shake my head. 'Not happening. Enjoy.'

'Fine,' she snaps, before turning away and heading toward the beach.

I would rather box-dye my hair than do yoga with those plebs. And I can't believe Kitty is joining them. Where is her loyalty? She's supposed to be supporting me. She hasn't asked if I'm ready for my sessions today or debriefed about dinner last night or the different people in the group. I want her to enjoy herself but she also needs to remember her place.

Before I head to breakfast I give Tom and the kids a call. I didn't say goodnight to the kids last night because I was at dinner. It's not the first time it's happened and it won't be the last—it's part of my job. Apparently, it's a part that Tom doesn't understand. We argue about it all the time. My priorities are, according to him, out of order. But I'm sure they're all enjoying a weekend in the resort-style pool we had put in a few summers ago or at all the sporting activities they participate in. All of those things are paid for by my book and the work I'm doing.

'Hello,' Tom answers after a few rings and his face appears on FaceTime.

'Hello. Are the kids up?'

'Yep. Just got Ava ready for ballet and Jack is grabbing his basketball shoes.' He turns away for a moment and calls out to them. 'How are you?'

I sigh. 'I'm alright.'

'Can't be too bad,' Tom says. 'You were out socialising last night and I saw Kitty post a photo to Instagram of the sunrise this morning.'

I can tell from his tone that this is him questioning my priorities again. 'I didn't join Kitty for the sunrise. I'm working, remember?'

The kids rush in behind Tom and lean in so that they can get their faces on the screen. Saved by the kids. That was another argument brewing. It's ironic that I have made my fortune on helping people find happiness within their marriages or giving them the courage to leave unhappy marriages, while my own marriage is in a downward spiral. Maybe I'm a fraud.

'Hi, Mummy,' Ava says. 'Daddy did my ballet bun today.'

I lean closer to the screen to inspect the bun, it's surrounded by bumps and fly aways. Miss Laura will not be pleased. My cheeks flush at the thought of other dance mums seeing that mess.

'Lovely, honey,' I force myself to say. 'Perhaps you can get to class a little early and ask Miss Laura to fix it up.'

Tom rolls his eyes. Usually, I'm home to at least do the dance bun. He'll be taking that personally. But I can't have my children in public like that.

'Are you excited for basketball, Jack?' I ask, ignoring Tom's glare.

'Mmm. Yeah. But yesterday at school, Lucas said that I was the worst in the team.'

A spark of fury passes through my body. I'm not totally cold-hearted—when my kids hurt, I hurt. He's six years old. He's no LeBron James but he tries so hard and practises at home every day. I even had a half court with a hoop concreted in the backyard so he could train.

I look to Tom for reassurance that he'll deal with the little pipsqueak who's picking on our son. I don't expect Tom to push the kid flat on his shit-talking face—as much as he deserves it—but he could mention something to the coach or his parents. Tom nods and I try to push down the feelings of protective anger. Knowing the other mums at basketball, Tom will probably give this kid's mum a heads up and she'll gush and smile apologetically while stroking his toned arm for a little longer than appropriate.

'Okay, kids,' Tom says, 'we need to keep moving. Say bye to Mummy.'

A chorus of byes come down the phone and they wave.

The call cuts off.

I begin scrolling on social media and see the photo that Tom was talking about. Kitty is doing a perfect headstand in front of a stunning beach sunrise. She should've been here helping me prepare. I'm going to have to speak to her.

Heading to breakfast, I'm so riled up. Between the lingering tension with Tom, and now Kitty, my son's bully and these dreaded counselling sessions, I'm almost considering taking myself to the poolside bar for shots rather than having breakfast with the guests. I keep trying to remind myself that this retreat is about business. It's about making myself relevant again, pushing for more followers and more sales. I'm not supposed to be having the time of my life.

Taking a deep breath, I enter the dining room and take a seat at one of the empty tables. There are a few guests here eating. Some of them nod hello but don't join me—thank goodness.

Molly approaches with a jug of water and a glass. 'Good morning, Ms Marsden. We have eggs benedict on sourdough this morning, as well as an assortment of fresh pastries, meats and cheeses. You can help yourself to those over there.' She points to a trestle table by the far wall. 'Would you like me to put through an order for eggs now?'

'Yes, please,' I say. I had put eggs benedict down as one of my preferred breakfast meals, so I'm pleased with the menu.

Another waitress brings me a coffee and I'm just about to take that first heavenly sip when Lachy sits down in the empty seat next to me.

'Is this seat taken?' he asks but he's already made himself comfortable before I can answer and the truth is, it's not taken.

'Not at all,' I mumble.

'Looking forward to our session later,' he says.

I force a smile. 'Yes, it will be great to get to know everyone a little better.'

He nods. 'I'm interested to hear your take on my marriage. Well, broken marriage. It came out of the blue and I think there was one thing that really stood out.'

At this moment, Kitty approaches looking fresh and zen in a long white shirt over a bikini. Lachy looks up at her.

'Oh, sorry. Here, sit down.'

He gets up and Kitty thanks him before taking the chair.

'Anyway, see you soon, Ms Marsden,' Lachy says, before walking away.

'You really missed out this morning, Ceels.'

I take a sip of my coffee. 'I needed to prepare for today. I'd hoped you might have helped me with it.'

'How can I help? I don't work with couples and I don't know anything about these people.'

She has a point but I'm still annoyed. 'Mmm. Well, a bit of moral support would be nice.'

'You can be so difficult, Celia, seriously. I'm going to get some croissants. You want anything?'

I shake my head. I'm tempted to tell her to go and sit with some of her yoga buddies and leave me in peace. After Lachy and her, I just want to be left alone.

I'm about to take the first bite of my breakfast, the poached eggs cooked to perfection, their runny yolks mixing with the hollandaise sauce, when Nadia storms into the dining room. I remember her from yesterday quite clearly. Partly because she is stunningly beautiful and partly because she was joined at the hip to another single guest, Tanner. I'd never explicitly said in any of the introductory emails or at the welcome meeting that the singles shouldn't hook up, but I hinted at it and I thought it was somewhat implied when they signed up for this retreat that they were here to better themselves not to meet someone else. Either way, their obvious attraction to one another piqued my interest and bugged me a little.

Nadia looks around the dining room, a piece of paper in her hands, and stops when she sees me. She doesn't look happy. She doesn't have the face of someone who enjoyed yoga at sunrise. I guess she missed it too.

She charges towards me.

'What the hell is this?' she yells, and slams the paper down next to me.

'Excuse me?' I say, standing up so that I'm eye level with her. Nobody speaks to me like that.

She picks up the note and waves it in front of my face. 'This note. How dare you.'

'Nadia, I suggest you lower your voice and calm down,' I say.

'Don't tell me what to do. You broke into my room!'

I scrunch up my face. 'What?'

Molly comes rushing over, while the rest of the dining room watches on.

'Nadia, please stop yelling,' Molly says, her face panicked as she glances around the room. 'We haven't had a chance to speak with Ms Marsden yet.'

'Speak to me about what?' I ask. *What the hell is going on?*

'Nadia's room was broken into last night and she found a note.'

I take the note from Nadia now and read it.

You're not here to meet someone. Do the right thing. -CM

I laugh. 'You think I left you this?'

'It's your initials,' Nadia says, her voice venomous.

'So? Anyone could've written that. It's not like it's my signature or bloody fingerprint. I assure you, I was in my own room all night.'

'Can you prove it?'

'No. Because like you, I'm here alone. And whilst I don't care enough about your love life to send you a note, I do agree that you aren't here to meet someone.'

'See! She agrees with what it says,' Nadia says, to no one in particular, as though she's just proved her point.

'Yes. Because I designed this retreat to help singles be comfortable being single. Not to provide the new setting of *Bachelor in Paradise*.'

'Nadia,' Molly says. 'We will look into this further. In the meantime, Greg will arrange extra security around the resort. Come and enjoy some breakfast.'

Nadia walks away, her head shaking, following Molly to a table.

Kitty takes her seat at the table, her eyes wide. 'So, did you write the note?' she asks, her lips curling up.

'Piss off, Kitty,' I say, and leave the dining room.

Chapter 13

Molly

My phone buzzes again. *Shit. Shit. Shit.* It'll be another tag on Instagram.

The Sand & Salt social media accounts are linked to my phone and it has been going off this morning. But not in a good way. No. The Sand & Salt Resort was the setting for an altercation between screaming guest, Nadia, and famous influencer, Celia Marsden.

Other guests had recorded the verbal stoush and it was being shared a thousand times over. We'd gone viral. Not the good kind of viral.

Instead, we were being outed as having lax security and not looking after our guests. After everything I have done to make sure this weekend goes ahead without a hitch, and something like this happens. Here I was worried about a meal preference or how soft the sheets were or the stupid napkin origami. And my real issue was security. Someone had broken into a guest's room. It was a nightmare.

Nadia had called reception late last night and Greg and I had calmed her down so that she could get some sleep. We told her we'd talk to Celia in the morning but before we'd even had a chance to, she let the whole dining room in on it, and by doing so the whole world as well. I don't know how I am going to rectify this situation.

This time the phone rings. I look at the call display. Joseph. The owner. My boss.

I take a deep breath and answer.

'Hey, Joey,' I say cheerfully, pretending my world isn't crumbling around me, hoping he hasn't heard the news.

'Molly, what's going on there? My daughter just called me and said people are fighting in my dining room and it's all over the internet.'

Dammit.

'Umm, yeah. There has been an incident but I assure you it's nothing to worry about,' I lie.

'I thought you said this event would be great for publicity. This wasn't the kind of publicity I had in mind.'

'No, of course not. Neither did I. There's just been a misunderstanding. It'll be fine, Joey. I promise.'

I can imagine him pulling at his long curly beard, a habit he always does when he is thinking or worried.

'I'm in the States at the moment so I can't get there to help fix this.'

'Of course but it's under control.' The lies keep on coming. Not only is Nadia still furious—and rightfully so—I have no idea who left that note and now Celia is pissed off at being publicly accused of breaking and entering. Things are far from under control.

'Okay. I'm trusting you. I'll call again tonight.'

'Sure thing. Bye.'

I hang up the phone and put my head in my hands. I don't know how I'm going to turn this around.

Chapter 14

Nadia

When I leave the dining room, I'm still furious. I storm back to my room with a danish from the breakfast spread. I'd have rather stayed and had a feast but I could feel the burn of everyone's eyes on me. I can't believe Molly hadn't spoken to Celia straight away, instead letting her tuck in to her eggs first. Is a break and enter not a big deal to them around here? Was guest safety not a priority?

Entering my room, I carefully open the door so that I don't knock over the lamp I left behind it. My amateur attempt at security. If it got knocked over, it would smash and I'd know if my late night visitor had been back. Thankfully, the lamp is intact.

I slump on the bed, stuffing the sticky pastry into my mouth when my phone rings. It's the third time my mother has tried to call me this morning. I don't want to answer and explain to her that her favourite author-turned-influencer is actually a psycho bitch but three calls stir a little worry in me.

'Hey, Mum,' I answer with a mouthful of food.

'Nadia, thank God, you're okay. What on earth is going on?'

Wait, what? How does she know someone came into my room. I purposely didn't call to tell her last night because I knew she'd worry herself sick. The only other people who know are...

'Nadia? Are you there? I've seen the videos. Are you arguing with Celia Marsden?'

Of course. Someone in that dining room, hell everyone in that dining room probably, had their phone out to film me as I confronted Celia.

'Yes, I'm here. Everything is fine. There was just a misunderstanding.'

'Darling, that woman is there to help you. You looked very, umm, aggressive.'

Are my ears deceiving me or is she taking Celia's side?

'Someone broke into my room, Mum.' I'm not going to let my own mum turn against me. She can know the truth. 'There was a note signed CM and I confronted her about it.'

'Oh my goodness. Are you okay? I'll pick you up today.'

'No, it's fine. I'm not leaving. You paid a fortune for me to be here. And they've said they'll increase their security.'

'We don't care about the money. Are you safe? Did Celia really do that?'

'I'm fine, Mum, honest. She says she didn't but who knows?'

'Well, you focus on you and feeling better. I'll be there to pick you up Monday.'

We exchange goodbyes and I swallow the rest of my breakfast.

This morning, the singles have free time while Celia conducts couples therapy sessions. Then, this afternoon, she meets with each of the singles.

It's so warm outside already and I'd love to just sit by the pool drinking cocktails but drinks before nine am is probably not recommended on a retreat where you're trying to improve your wellbeing.

I throw on a bikini with some denim shorts and a pink shirt and head to the pool. Just as I open my door to leave, lamp in place, I come face to face with Tanner. I'd almost forgotten about him with everything going on. I haven't even told him about the note yet, although he's probably seen social media like everyone else.

'Hey,' he says, smiling and instantly relieving some of my tension.

'Hi.'

'Where are you headed?'

I shrug. 'Not sure yet. Was going to sit by the pool and work it out from there.'

'Can I interest you in some paddle boarding?' he asks.

My insides squeeze. Physical activity, no thanks. I may look extremely thin, but it's not from exercise and I'm as weak as they come. But what else am I going to do? Sit by the pool and get more pissed off about that note? Embarrassing myself on a paddle board sounds far more appealing.

'Sure,' I say. 'But I haven't done it before.'

'That's okay. There are beginner boards in the shed near the pool and I can teach you.'

I pull my front door closed and double check it's locked, twisting the handle several times to be sure. Then we head to the pool shed.

I manage to stand on my paddle board for a grand total of three seconds. Simply kneeling and paddling past the break in the waves leaves me exhausted and I can tell that my arms will be so sore tomorrow that I probably won't be able to wash my hair.

After about half an hour of attempting to stand up, wobbling on the spot and falling into the salty water before climbing back on the board and repeating it all again, I give up.

'You'll just have to come on my board instead,' Tanner says, and I raise my eyebrows.

I would be quite happy to be paddled around, Venetian style. Me, pretending to be in my parents' distant homeland and Tanner my sexy gondolier.

My dreams are dashed quite quickly. Tanner wasn't thinking of making his paddle board a gondola for me to ride upon. He wants me to practise standing up.

'I hope you're prepared to get wet,' I say, and he winks.

I look away, hoping he doesn't see my cheeks flush.

Once we're in the calm water, Tanner stands up behind me and steadies himself before reaching down to take one of my hands.

My knees wobble as he helps me to my feet. Somehow he uses his legs to counteract the movements mine make so that we stay balanced. He's standing just inches behind me, I can feel his breath on my neck, which does nothing to stop my body from shaking.

'You're doing great,' he whispers in my ear.

He begins to paddle and our board glides across the water slowly. My arms are out, aeroplane style, and I cringe at how ridiculous I must look.

Then a Jet Ski flies past, sending a ripple past our board and my legs can't handle it. I must look like a baby giraffe taking its first steps as my legs threaten to give way beneath me. Tanner laughs, then grabs me around the waist and pulls me into the water.

My head breaks through the surface and there's Tanner grinning at me.

'Hey,' I say. 'You pulled me in.'

'I didn't think you were going to recover from that one. Best to make an elegant dismount.'

I smile, wiping my hair from my eyes. 'Elegant is a stretch.'

He helps me back onto the board and I sit down, one leg on either side. He sits behind me, straddling the board too.

'Hey, turn around,' he says.

I awkwardly shift around on my butt so that I'm facing him. We sit there, the board rocking gently and the sun beaming down on us. It's perfect.

'Glad you came paddle boarding then?' he asks.

I nod. 'It definitely improved my mood.' The drama of the note and Celia had shifted momentarily from the front of my mind.

'Why? What's wrong?'

What's wrong? Is he kidding? Surely he knows. Everyone at the resort knows. Everyone with social media knows.

'You know? The note and my run in with Celia?'

He shifts himself closer. Our knees are touching and my skin tingles where they meet.

'What are you talking about?'

'You haven't seen Instagram or heard from anyone?'

'I don't use social media. Find it's safer as a cop. And I slept late this morning after our night together. You're the first person I saw.'

Part of me is relieved he doesn't know. I wish I hadn't said anything and then we could've just continued enjoying this moment. But the other part of me is nervous because now I have to be the one to tell him.

'When I got back to my room last night, I discovered someone had been in there. They'd moved some things and they left a note.'

His eyes widen. 'What? Why didn't you come and get me?'

It was a fair question. I don't really know the answer. But I'd just met him and I didn't think it would be appropriate to be his damsel in distress.

I shrug.

'Well, what did the note say?'

'"You're not here to meet someone. Do the right thing." And then it had the initials C.M.'

Tanner's face reddens. 'What the hell! Someone is keeping tabs on us. And who's C.M?' It takes him a second and his jaw drops. 'Not Celia, surely?'

'Well, I thought so but when I confronted her at breakfast, she denied it.'

'Nadia,' he says, placing a hand on my thigh and sending my heart rate through the roof. 'I'm so sorry. I can't believe this. Have you reported it?'

'I told Molly and Greg. They said they'll increase security. It's all they can do, really.'

'Well, then we'll call the police. I know a few guys in the NSW Police Force that I could reach out to.'

'It's okay,' I say, placing my hand over his. He turns his hand over so that it's holding mine now and gives it a gentle squeeze. 'I'm just going to focus on the retreat. No need for police.'

He pulls his hand away. 'Okay, if you're sure. But you let me know if I can help or if I should back off.'

I close my eyes for a moment. I didn't mean that focus on the retreat meant not hanging out with him and doing whatever this is. But I also don't think I can cope with more notes. When I open my eyes, my decision is made. There's something different about this guy. I cross my legs so that I can move even closer to him, between his legs.

'I don't want you to back off.'

He leans in and kisses me. Just once and so softly. I run my tongue over my lips, tasting the salty water from his, longing for more. But I think Tanner is just as aware as me that we're in public and someone is watching us.

Chapter 15

Jocelyn

'Andy,' I call out, 'look at this.'

He comes out of the bathroom, his expression as though I've asked for a kidney. I'm just that much of a burden.

'What?' His tone matches his expression and I wish now that I'd said nothing.

We have barely spoken since our argument by the pool. He told me I need to focus on us and yet he has basically pretended I don't exist.

I realise that what I want to show him is exactly the kind of thing that'll piss him off even more. I don't know why I even thought to show him.

'Never mind,' I say, and smile, hoping to warm the freezing tension between us.

He just goes straight back into the bathroom while I continue to scroll through footage of that single chick, Nadia, having an argument with Celia in the dining room. I'm dying to know more.

Our couples therapy session with Celia couldn't come at a better time. Although I worry that our current silent treatment is going to make the session awkward and pointless.

I try to push down my fangirl feelings when I see Celia and remember why I'm here. It's not to snap photos or be her best friend. I'm here for Andy. For our marriage. For our unborn children.

Celia sits in a dark green armchair across from a brown leather couch. A round glass coffee table separates the chairs and is topped with a jug of water, glasses, a fresh bunch of flowers and tissues. *Yikes. That's presumptuous.*

Andy and I take a seat on the couch—no part of our bodies touching, several inches of clear, tense air between us. I imagine an episode of *Married at First Sight* and what the body language "experts" would say about our positions. "Clearly there's something up with these two." *Well done, geniuses.*

'Jocelyn and Andy, welcome,' Celia says. Her voice is strange. It's soft and calming. It doesn't match the confident, almost sassy, influencer vibe she usually gives off. Perhaps this is her therapist voice. It irks me to be honest. 'Why don't you tell me what brought you on this retreat.'

I glance at Andy, whose eyes are locked on Celia.

Okay then. I guess I'll go. I clear my throat. 'Firstly, thank you for meeting with us.' I sense Andy shift beside me. 'Andy and I have been trying to get pregnant for a while now and it's taking a toll on our relationship. I expressed perhaps taking a break from trying to conceive and Andy doesn't agree.'

'What? Jocelyn, are you kidding me? You told me *yesterday* that you wanted to take a break. We booked this retreat months ago because we wanted to work on our relationship *while* we are still trying to conceive.'

My cheeks redden. *Way to throw me under the bus, jerk.*

Celia just nods and scribbles in a notebook.

Andy continues, 'I think sometimes Joss hasn't got her priorities in order.'

Now it's my turn to cut him off. 'Excuse me! Don't talk to me about my priorities. Everything I do is about trying to make a baby. The vitamins, the tracking, the ovulation sticks, the pregnancy tests, keeping fit, eating the right things. I'm exhausted.'

'Now, now,' Celia says, and my shoulders tense at her voice. 'Let Andy explain.'

Is she kidding? He's allowed to cut me off and now I'm being told to shush like a naughty kid in class.

'I just think Joss worries about what other people are doing or thinking more than she worries about us.'

Celia nods and my cheeks burn even hotter. I'm sweating and can feel my legs sticking to the leather couch. I can't believe this is happening.

Before anyone speaks again, there's a knock on the door and Molly enters without being asked.

Celia's face hardens and I'm glad I'm not Molly because if looks could kill.

'Ms Marsden, I'm so sorry to interrupt.' She glances at us and gives an apologetic smile. 'But I wanted to let you know that Nadia is not going to the police. You don't need to worry.'

Celia's eyes widen and I'm sure fireballs are about to shoot out of them onto Molly. 'Of course I needn't worry. I've done nothing wrong,' she hisses.

'Of course,' Molly says quickly. 'I just wanted to update you.'

'Well, perhaps not while I'm in a therapy session. Please close the door behind you.'

Molly scurries away and my mind is racing. Nadia was going to call the police. What the hell had Celia done?

I struggle to concentrate for the remainder of the session. Partly because I was already pissed off that Celia sided early with Andy and partly because something was going down at this retreat and I was dying to know what.

When we get back to our room, Andy gives me a hug and I melt into it. I'm not interested in arguing with him.

Somewhere in the muffled voices that spoke around me and not to me in there, we'd agreed to keep trying for two more months and then take a break. A compromise. *Sure*, I'd said.

Twitter Excerpt

Tweet from @CeliaMarsdenTherapy

March 30th, 2020

How's your balance between 'Me Time' and 'We Time'? Share your thoughts! How much time do you dedicate to your hobbies and quality moments with your partner? Let's hear your tips for maintaining that sweet spot! #SelfCare #Relationships #QualityTime

Comments:

@Lovelost: @CeliaMarsdenTherapy my husband is addicted to video games. How do I talk to him about spending more time with me?

@CeliaMarsdenTherapy: @Lovelost honesty is best. Talk to him about something you both enjoy that you can do together

@AnnieCho: Sorry to hijack your comment @Lovelost. @CeliaMarsdenTherapy my partner and I both enjoy video games but I find that doing this together is actually making things worse. Like we just play and ignore each other.

@CeliaMarsdenTherapy: @AnnieCho this is quite common. We hear about this with couples who play golf, are gaming, even reading. Perhaps an activity with a shared goal—home improvement, gardening, exercise?

@Lovelost: Thanks @CeliaMarsdenTherapy and good luck @AnnieCho

Chapter 16

Celia

The morning of couples therapy had gone pretty well, I think. I mean everyone pissed me off beyond words but then that happens all the time, whatever I'm doing. The couples left happy and with goals, and I was proud of myself. I still had it.

Next I have the singles, which is more out of my comfort zone. Working with couples had been my passion leading up to writing my book. But I'd advertised this as an opportunity for singles too. Really, they have to do most of the work and they've already all filled out an online questionnaire about their history and lifestyle so I have a pretty good idea of where to start with a lot of them.

First up on my list is Tanner. Not an ideal place to start since he is directly involved with the drama that's unfolded so far. But at least I'm not starting with Nadia who actually cancelled her session earlier this morning. *What does that even mean? She's just here for a holiday now?*

Tanner's profile reads that he's a police officer whose wife left him because she came second to the job. He became depressed, turned to alcohol, and his job and relationships turned to shit. Textbook stuff really.

There's a soft knock on the door and Tanner comes in, taking a seat on the leather couch. He looks tense as he looks across at me, his hair tucked under a cap and dripping onto his white t-shirt.

'Been swimming today?' I ask, breaking the ice.

He nods. 'Paddle boarding. Lost track of time actually.'

'Lovely. So, tell me why you signed up for the retreat.'

I get a welcome fifteen minute break before my last few singles sessions. I feel as though I've run a marathon and sat the Mensa IQ test. My brain and body hurt. A combination of working through these people's problems and tensing my body so as to hide my frustration and disgust with them.

Some of them are absolutely lost causes. In life and love.

Kitty joins me for a quick cup of tea after having apologised to me about the note earlier.

'So, how was your first day back on the couch?' she asks.

'I'm going to need something much stronger,' I say, holding up the mug.

'That bad?'

'It wasn't bad. It's just not my thing anymore. I struggle to empathise like I used to.'

'No shit. I could've told you that.'

I shoot a warning glare. I'm not in the mood for more of her snarky comments.

'It's all just arguments about hours spent on the golf course, dollars spent on the roulette table and then one girl who wants to take a break from trying for a baby with her drop-dead-gorgeous husband who desperately wants a child with the love of his life. The woman doesn't know how great she's got it.'

'Come on, Celia. Fertility is a touchy subject.'

'Yeah, I know but who wouldn't want to bone that guy just for fun anyway. Girl's got rocks in her head.'

'Definitely low on the empathy,' Kitty says, under her breath but loud enough for me to hear.

I let it go. I'm not in the mood for any more arguments.

'How many more to go?' she asks.

'Just two,' I say. 'Wish me luck. And have a cocktail ready.'

Chapter 17

Molly

'I've actually been here a few times,' Lachy says, 'back when I was married.'

Despite the guests having so many incredible activities at their disposal during free time, Lachy has decided to spend his free time talking to me as I fold napkins in the dining room. I'd have thought my focus on work would deter him and he'd eventually leave but no. He doesn't need the conversation to be reciprocal. He seems quite happy to do all the talking.

'Do you remember us?' he asks.

I'm about to answer, possibly my first contribution to the conversation when he continues.

'Probably not. You must get lots of guests through here. Such a beautiful resort.'

'Thank you,' I manage during a pause in his monologue.

'But yeah, then my wife left me and I haven't been back. What a great reason to return. Celia Marsden. My wife loved her too. Well, probably still does. I haven't spoken to her recently. I'm sure she'd be so jealous to know I met Celia. She was obsessed with that book.'

I nod and glance around the dining room. Still so much to prepare before dinner and this guy just won't leave. I try to send telepathic messages to Greg to come and save me. *Stupid, I know.* I even throw a few "save me" looks in Carlos' direction but he doesn't understand and just smiles.

The door to the dining room opens and Greg walks in. Maybe I am telepathic. Although the frown on his face suggests I probably don't want to know why he's here.

'Molly, can I have a word?'

I turn to Lachy. 'Why don't you go and enjoy the sunshine. I highly recommend the local beer.'

'Is that the Stone & Wood? My wife and I used to visit the brewery regularly. Did I mention we're local to the Northern Rivers.'

'No, I didn't realise,' I say, getting frustrated.

Greg must sense it. 'Try the pale ale, mate, it's perfect on a day like this.'

Lachy finally takes the hint and leaves the dining room.

'What's going on?' I ask.

'Another guest has had a break in. A couple this time. Mr and Mrs Lambert.'

My stomach drops picturing the older couple, both with grey hair and sporting golf attire, even at mealtimes. 'What?'

'Yeah. They went into town today after their session with Celia and when they got back this afternoon, their golf clubs had been, um, *tampered* with.'

'What the hell does that mean?'

'Apparently, there's an order to these things and a wood was where an iron should be or something. Personally, I've never taken to the sport but you know, golfers take this stuff pretty seriously.'

I knit my brows together. 'Are they sure they didn't just put them back in the wrong place?'

'No, they're adamant. Plus, their door was ajar when they returned.'

'Okay, Greg, what is going on?'

He shrugs. 'Seems like someone is trying to scare some of our guests.'

'But why? And why aren't they taking stuff?'

'It seems like they're just trying to send a message.'

'Okay, so what is this message?'

Greg rubs his eyebrows. 'The Lamberts said that during their session, Celia suggested they take a step back from golf to find other things they enjoy together. So they did, they went for a big walk into town. Then they came back to the clubs being messed with.'

'They think Celia did it?'

'To them, it's the only thing that makes sense.'

I sigh. Why? Why? Why did I sign up for this?

There were several Tripadvisor reviews suggesting Sand & Salt would be great to host a retreat. One even went as far as mentioning Celia by name, saying they thought she should do a couples retreat.

The idea seemed alright and we were really struggling. I'd reached out to Megan, Celia's manager, and she had planned the rest.

'It won't be just for couples,' Megan had said, when she'd agreed. 'We'll invite singles, too, because Celia has helped so many people bravely leave their marriages.'

Boy do I regret it now.

'So, what should we do?' I ask Greg.

'I'll ask around and chat to Celia but I don't think we'll get any answers and the Lamberts aren't interested in going to the police.'

'Let me speak with Celia,' I say. 'You find out if anyone saw anything unusual.'

I look down at the swan napkin in my hand and want to rip its head off. Why is this happening?

Chapter 18
Jocelyn

After our session, Andy announces that he's going surfing.

'You don't know how to surf,' I say.

'I'm getting a lesson down at the beach.'

'Oh, awesome. What do we need to bring?'

'We?'

Yes we. Why not we? Surely he isn't going without me. 'I want to learn too.'

He walks over to me and gives me a hug—not a warm, loving husband hug; more like the awkward ones you give when you're thirteen and just saw your friend at a party.

'Joss, I thought it might be good for us to do a separate activity this afternoon.'

'This is a couples retreat.'

Andy nods. 'Yes, but it's also for individuals to discover things about themselves.'

'So hang on a sec. You say I'm distracted and not dedicated because I have a cocktail or indulge in some harmless gossip but you want to go out surfing without me. Doesn't sound very dedicated to our marriage, Andy.'

He rolls his eyes. 'Don't be so dramatic. It's two hours max. Go and have a cocktail, read a book by the pool. You love that sort of thing.'

I purse my lips and raise my eyebrows. 'Sure.'

When I get to the pool, there's only one lounge available. I had hoped it wouldn't be too busy down here so I could avoid eye contact and small talk and not give away the fact that I'm pissed off and hurt.

I use the QR code on the table next to my lounge to order a lemon drop and some fries. Probably not approved for someone who's meant to be *trying*. The word makes my ears burn. I felt so ganged up on in our session with Celia. I don't know how it happened but Andy got his way. I was unheard. Disrespected. And yet, this is my body.

'What are you ordering?' a voice asks from the lounge next to me.

I turn to see Lachy, one of the singles, AirPods in his ears. Hopefully that's a sign he won't want to chat. I fish around in my bag, looking for my own headphones. Andy is always teasing me for losing them in my bag.

'Just a cocktail and fries.'

'Nice. Just ordered a drink myself. How did you find your session with Celia?'

So much for not chatting. Plus, isn't that kind of private?

'Yeah, not bad. Have you had yours?'

He looks at his watch. 'Not for another hour and five. Very interested to hear what she says.'

I finally find the headphones and make a point of putting them in my ears. 'Hopefully, she can help you with whatever you need.'

'I doubt it. I want to know how she feels about being the reason my wife, Louisa, left me.'

My eyes widen and I'm thankful my sunglasses hide my reaction.

'You're really going to ask her that?'

'That's why I came. I think she needs to know she's hurting people.'

'Look, I don't know anything about your marriage but I assume your wife left you for her own reasons that were probably there long before she read the book.'

Lachy's eyes narrow and for the first time I notice how light they are. Ice blue. But not in a stunning Swedish supermodel way, in a *Game of Thrones* Night King I'm-going-to-kill-you way.

'You know nothing about my wife,' he snaps.

Then he picks up his towel and leaves.

Weirdo.

I desperately try to get into my audiobook—a grumpy sunshine rom-com, how ironic. But I can't stop thinking about Andy. I've never seen him get so frustrated with me like this. Our life has always been so easy. We travel lots, we have a nice house, we go to the gym together— push each other to go faster or heavier—and we laugh so much. A baby will change everything. It already is and it hasn't even been conceived yet.

I sip my cocktail and begin scrolling Instagram instead. It's been a few hours but those videos of Nadia yelling at Celia are still popping up all over my feed. I recognise the original poster of the video. One of the single older women. Based on my few conversations with her, I imagine this is her first time going viral and I also imagine she has no idea what that means.

I click on the comments below her video.

Gary Kipp: My money's on the brunette. Celia has no chance

Susie Delpolta: I've seen Celia do boxing at the local gym. @Gary Kipp don't write her off

Macca: @Susie Delpolta that's kind of creepy

I keep scrolling. There's a lot of *who would win* and *what happened next* and speculation about whether Celia really wrote some note.

A recent comment catches my eye. Posted a few minutes ago.

Jezza M: There's more than meets the eye here. This retreat has been managed terribly.

The comment insinuates that the writer of it is at the retreat. I still don't really know what happened with Nadia this morning but the fact that there's more to it seems alarming. Also, who is this Jezza M who seems to be in the know? And what note? I couldn't find any details of it in the comments I read through.

After an hour of more scrolling, I head back to our room. Hopefully, Andy will be done with his surf lesson. Part of me hopes he got wiped out several times. When I get to the door, it's wide open. He must be inside, along with the hundred flies he's letting in. He does this all the time at home, too, leaving doors open and letting in all the bugs. I'm not going to say anything though. It'll just be another argument and I really don't think I can handle more time apart from Andy.

'Babe,' I call. He's probably in the shower. I close the front door and head for the bathroom but there's no sound of running water. The door is closed so I knock. 'Andy, are you in there?'

Nothing.

My heart rate rises a little.

I open the door to the bathroom. The first thing I see is the shower—empty. As I open the door wider, the rest of the bathroom comes into view. On the bathroom vanity is a note and a small box. I glance around the bathroom. Everything else is in place.

Maybe, this is a little game that Andy is playing to spice things up again. My body warms thinking about him. Perhaps, he's trying to find that spark we've been lacking a bit lately. Gosh, I hope he pops out in a moment wearing nothing but whipped cream.

I pick up the note.

Stop taking your husband for granted. Use this properly and give him what he wants.

My blood turns to ice. *What the hell!* I drop the note and pick up the package. It's wrapped in a napkin, like the ones from the dining room.

I unfold the napkin and find a box of ovulation sticks.

My cheeks burn. I don't know whether to feel angry, terrified or completely violated that someone has been in our room and done this. All of the above, I guess.

I read the note again. *Stop taking your husband for granted.* How could they say that? Because despite our fertility issues, anyone who knows me, knows that I worship that man. He's my dream guy, my perfect opposite. Tears start to fall and before long I'm sobbing into the napkin wrapping paper.

Andy returns from the beach and finds me crying on the bed. In the half an hour since I found the note, many emotions have made their way through me. Fear, that someone was in our room. Sadness, that someone thinks I'm not worthy. Anger, that I've been given ovulation tests. I hadn't been able to pull myself together enough to even call Andy and ask him to come back or for me to report the break in.

When Andy gets to the end of the bed, I have well and truly entered the anger phase. He sits down next to me and places an arm around my shoulders.

I push him away. 'Was it you?' I scream, tears still falling.

'What's going on, Joss? Are you okay?'

'Just tell me, did you leave the note?'

'What note?' he says, shifting on the bed.

'This.' I thrust it towards his body.

He looks at it for a moment, frowning. 'Jocelyn, who gave you this?'

'I found it in the bathroom.'

'Was there anything else?'

I storm into the bathroom and return with the box of ovulation tests. I stand in front of him and hold them up. I say nothing.

Andy's eyes narrow, taking in the box. He probably has no idea what they even are. I'm the one that has to take care of all this side of it.

'They're ovulation tests. They tell a woman when she's ovulating. Apparently, I'm not using them properly.' Then I burst into tears, again.

Andy jumps up off the bed and pulls me into him. He strokes my hair out of my eyes until he can see my face. 'Joss, look at me.'

I blink away some tears before looking up. His eyes are warm but something behind them is burning, raging.

'Babe, I didn't leave you that note. You know I'd never do that.'

Deep down, of course I know that. The guy doesn't even get angry when his football team is losing or when the same telemarketer calls during dinner for the third night in a row. He's a grump at times but he doesn't get aggressive or threatening, it's just not him. However, whatever is burning inside him right now is brand new. His body is tense and he's clenching his jaw so hard, I worry his teeth might break.

I nod. 'Someone's been in our room then.'

He pulls me back against him and squeezes me. 'I'm so sorry. I should've been here.'

I open my mouth to say it's okay. But I'm not okay with it. Regardless of the note and someone coming into our room, he should never have left me. We're on a couples retreat.

'Joss, have you told anyone here that we're trying?'

Oh, here we go again. He has an issue with my big mouth. I pull away from him.

'For your information,' I say, my tone harsh. 'I haven't spoken to anyone about why we're here.'

'Whoa,' he says, hands up. 'I'm just trying to narrow down who it could be. I'm not mad at you.'

'Well, that's a change.'

He sits on the bed and pulls me on top of him. I can't help it I love snuggling into his lap. My little place where I always feel safe.

'Jocelyn, that note is bullshit. I've got everything I want right here in my arms.'

I smile and new tears fall.

'But someone knows we've been having issues and they're threatening you. The only person who knows is Celia.'

I spring to my feet. 'She was accused of leaving a note for Nadia too.'

What the hell? Was this woman a psycho? Is this her method of therapy? Scare her patients or threaten her patients into doing what she thinks is best. And what the hell does she know anyway.

'We need to find Nadia,' I say and I wait for Andy to groan about this not being an "us" activity or it being a chance to gossip. Instead he nods.

'One thing first, though.' His eyes darken and his mouth curls up. 'You know I love you, babe.'

Then he sweeps me off my feet and lies me down on the bed. My heart races and my insides warm in anticipation. Nadia can wait. I need this.

Do they say break-up sex or make-up sex is better? I don't know. But I give a strong vote for the latter. Or the new "something absolutely horrifying happened let's distract ourselves with sex" sex. It was everything we needed. Finally, sex without the precursor of ovulation tests and without the pressure in the back of my mind.

When we go to find Nadia, we are both far too cheerful for people who have just had their room broken into and found a threatening note. But somehow it's brought us closer together. We're a team again.

Nadia is by the pool spending her free time the same way as she did yesterday—at the bar with Tanner.

I want to swoon over the potential romance unfolding but I also need to stay focussed and try and avoid a will-you-stop-gossiping eye roll from Andy.

He and I take a seat on two barstools, next to Nadia and Tanner. They smile when they see us.

'Hey,' I say. 'We haven't properly met. I'm Jocelyn and this is my husband Andy.'

She points to herself and then at him. 'Nadia and this is Tanner.'

'We need to talk to you,' my voice is more serious now. 'I found a note in my room this afternoon.'

Nadia flinches.

'Apparently, you did, too, and I wanted to ask you about it. See if it could have come from the same person.'

Nadia glances at Tanner who is no longer smiling.

'How do we know you're not just trying to get content for social media like everyone else?' he says. 'Nadia's mum is beside herself.'

I take my note out of my handbag and pass it to them. 'It came with a box of ovulation tests.'

Tanner's face flushes. 'I see. You should order a drink.'

Chapter 19

Nadia

C elia had been so adamant that she didn't leave the note in my room last night. I didn't believe her then and after seeing Jocelyn's note, I definitely don't believe her now. Celia is the only person on this retreat that knew about their fertility issues until now. They discussed it in the privacy of their session. Who else could it possibly be?

'Have you told Molly or Greg?' I ask, after Jocelyn recalls the details of finding the note. 'Because this is the second time someone's room has been broken into.'

'We've only told you,' Jocelyn says.

'I think we should call the cops,' Andy says.

'So does Tanner but I don't want to. He thought about reaching out to a mate but now he reckons it'll achieve nothing. There's no footage, no witnesses and because it's a resort, the amount of physical evidence all over the rooms is huge. You don't want to hear him rattle off the stats about hair and skin fibres in hotel rooms.' I'd almost vomited when Tanner explained it to me earlier.

Andy and Jocelyn look at each other. He puts an arm around her.

'What do we do?' Jocelyn asks.

I shrug. 'I don't know. I'm copping it on social media big time at the moment. Trolls are saying I'm aggressive and crazy. We have two more nights here. I'd say enjoy your holiday together and just avoid Celia.'

'It doesn't seem right,' Andy says.

'It's not,' I say. 'But we basically have two options. We can go home early. We don't get our money back. Or we can stay at the resort, just do our own thing and relax.'

There's no way I was going home early and facing my mother any sooner than necessary. Or the rest of society for that matter. I've become a villain somehow despite being the victim. I'm holding on to the fact that these things tend to blow over quickly so if I can spend a few extra days in a private resort, keeping my head down, I will.

There's a pause in the conversation and everyone sips quietly on their drinks.

Tanner clears his throat. 'I've got a better idea.'

Tanner walks me back to my room to get ready for dinner.

'I really don't know if I can go through with it,' I say, referring to the plan he'd just proposed.

Tanner suggested that we all attend Celia's Q&A session tonight and our therapy sessions tomorrow, pretending like nothing is wrong. He thinks if she's guilty, she'll assume we'll all avoid her but by attending, we might freak her out and she'll make a mistake. We'll get our proof. I don't think Celia gets rattled very easily so I'm not super confident in his plan.

'I know. After what she's put you through, you shouldn't have to sit one-on-one with her. But she'll be shocked when you arrive. You'll definitely be on the front foot.'

'But I have nothing to say. Do I pretend none of this happened and talk to her about my sad, single life?'

'If you can.'

We get to my front door and I invite him in, shifting the lamp aside. I struggle with a bottle opener and wine, my arms still sore from paddle boarding. He helps me get the wine open, I pour him some and we sit on the sofa in the living space of the small room.

'I don't know if I can pretend.' Plus, I'm not feeling miserable anymore. I had the most amazing day with Tanner. Paddle boarding, relaxing by the pool. The only time we weren't together was when Tanner went for his session with Celia and I really missed him.

'I know. She's an evil woman. If she didn't leave the note, why hasn't she checked up on you. You're one of her guests.'

Man, he's sweet. He hasn't stopped asking me if I'm okay all day. He even offered to sleep on the couch if I felt scared. That'd really set off the secret note writer.

'I can pretend none of the note stuff happened,' I say. I take a big swig of wine. Do I say it? To hell with it. I move closer to him on the sofa and turn to look at him properly. 'But I can't pretend to be a sad single anymore. I kind of like happy, single Nadia.'

Tanner smiles and closes the gap between us even more. 'People claimed Celia was going to heal us but I don't think she was the person I needed.'

We haven't kissed since our moment on the paddle boards when we were out in the open, for all to see. Now, I am acutely aware of the privacy we have. My curtains are drawn, the door is locked and I swear Tanner can probably hear my heartbeat.

'Who do you need?' I ask, my voice low and raspy.

Tanner leans in, his hand moves to my cheek and the warmth of it sends tingles all over my body.

I part my lips. Waiting, yearning. Gosh, I haven't been with a man in the longest time.

His lips meet mine and this time it isn't a soft peck. It's hard and needy. I open my mouth to let him in and his tongue sweeps through, my insides melting.

He pulls me onto his lap so I'm straddling him on the sofa. I'm still in my bikini and my skin burns as his fingers trace circles all over my back and stomach, teasing me.

He hardens below me. I press myself down against him and he moans.

Tanner moves from my lips and starts a line of kisses down my neck to my shoulder, where he slides off the strap to my bikini top.

A shrill ringing cuts into the moment. We pull apart, breathless.

I look at my phone on the table, lit up with the word "Mum". Bloody hell. She sure knows when to pick her moments.

I turn back to Tanner, pressing my lips to his but he pulls back.

'I hate myself for saying this but answer it, she's worried about you.'

I sigh. I get off him, slowly sliding a finger down his chest and torso until it reaches the top of his boardshorts. 'Stay there.'

I get off the phone to Mum who was just checking for the hun-dredth time if I was okay. I reassured her that I was now avoiding social media and I didn't need her to relay the contents of the death threats and hate speech from the Celia fans' comments.

When I return to the living space, Tanner is standing up.

'I thought I told you not to move,' I pout, moving closer to him. I place my hands on his chest and push up to kiss him.

He puts a finger to my lips. 'I heard some of the things your mum was saying. Sorry, I wasn't eavesdropping but you had her on speaker.'

I always put my mum on speaker. She tends to make phone conversations last far longer than necessary so I usually find a task to do while she speaks. Just now, I'd managed to straighten my hair.

He continues. 'Those comments are horrible, Nadia. Maybe we should be doing more about them.'

'No, I've already come round to your plan.' I slip my fingers just under the waistband of his shorts and his breath hitches.

'Dinner is in fifteen minutes. I want to be in the dining room and at the Q&A after. I want to say something.'

'I'm fine, Tanner. I don't care what those people say.'

'I do. I care about you.' He pecks me on the lips. 'I'll come get you in ten for dinner.' Then he leaves and my insides scream in frustration. I move the lamp back to the door and then flop onto the bed.

Loveless Marriage

Excerpt from the best-selling book by Celia Marsden

In previous chapters, the primary focus has been on assisting individuals and couples in finding happiness and fulfilment within their relationships. While the emphasis is always on promoting open communication, understanding and collaborative efforts to enhance a relationship, there are circumstances where remaining in the partnership may not be the most suitable course of action. It is essential to acknowledge that persisting in a relationship that consistently brings unhappiness, pain or harm can have adverse effects on one's mental and emotional well-being. In such situations, I believe that individuals should carefully consider their own happiness and overall quality of life. At times, the most prudent choice may involve parting ways and embarking on a journey toward personal growth and contentment, even if it necessitates the termination of a relationship. Ultimately, each scenario is unique, and individuals are encouraged to seek support in making decisions that are conducive to their well-being.

Chapter 20

Celia

You know the saying *save the best for last*? Well, imagine the best is a self-absorbed, idiotic middle-aged-man who doesn't listen and doesn't shut up.

My final session today was with Lachy. He's not here to find out how to be happy as a newly single man. No, he's here to pull my book apart and find out where he went wrong with his wife and how to fix it.

'Did you ask your ex-wife to join you on the retreat? I could've worked with you both.'

Not only did he ignore the question, but he got frustrated when I said I couldn't tell him why his wife left him because *I don't know his wife*.

When I finally finished with him—his session went twenty minutes over—I was about ready to walk into the ocean and never return.

I get back to my room and shower, washing off a day's worth of therapy, also known as a day of tears, arguments, self-discovery and tension—a lot of tension.

I'm doing my make-up for tonight's dinner and dreaded Q&A session when there's a knock at the door. *Bless, Kitty*. I bet she's here with that cocktail. I open the door and it's Greg.

'Oh,' I say when I see him.

'Sorry to bother you, Ms Marsden, but there's been another room break in. Nothing stolen but the guests are rattled.'

'Yes, I know. You've already asked me about Nadia, and her video attacking me is all over the internet.' Bloody hell. Why is he bringing it up again when Nadia says she's dropped it. And it wasn't me anyway.

'It's not just Nadia.'

My eyes narrow. 'What?'

'So, you don't know anything about it?' Greg asks. He's fidgeting with his watch, clearly nervous.

'Of course not. I don't know anything about any of this. You and Molly need to sort out the security at this place because this is tarnishing *my* reputation.'

'With all due respect, Ms Marsden, this is also tarnishing *our* reputation and we've never had an issue with security until this retreat started.'

My cheeks burn. What the hell is he insinuating? Does he know who I am? I could make or break this place with the click of a button.

'Anything else?' I ask, ready to close the door on him.

His lips twist like he's contemplating something more. Then he shakes his head. 'See you at dinner, Ms Marsden.'

I have never dreaded a public speaking event more than this and it is just to a room of thirty odd people, all of whom I've spoken with today—well, except Nadia.

But dinner was the cherry on top of my already faltering confidence. There were so many whispers, so many stares. I'd gone from people with a little stage fright around me to people actually being frightened of me. And I'd done absolutely nothing wrong.

Tonight is supposed to be an opportunity for people to ask about my book, to delve deeper into the topics I wrote about, but I could already predict that the questions were going to be far from book related.

The recreation room has been transformed again with the same makeshift lectern. Instead of rows of chairs, there are small tables surrounded by chairs, scattered around the space. It's a casual evening, where guests can have a drink and the chef is even preparing some after-dinner treats.

It's dark outside so the limited light I had the other day, during the welcome meeting, is now non-existent. And this time, I couldn't care less. I won't be sending Kitty to fetch my ring light or stressing about which angle casts a shadow on my face. I just want to get this over with. Plus, Kitty had told me she was opting for a night in anyway. Another questionable best friend move.

I place a copy of *Loveless Marriage* on the lectern. This time I don't have any notes, just blank paper and a pen. This evening is totally unscripted, however, I know this book inside out.

The door opens and Molly holds it open while Greg lugs in a big box.

'Hurry,' she says. I don't think I've ever seen Molly not flustered. 'Oh, Ms Marsden,' she says, when she sees me. 'You're early.'

'Just getting set up.'

'Lovely. Us too. Can I get you a drink?'

'Water would be great.'

Molly gives Greg a knowing look and he hurries off, presumably to fetch my drink.

'How was your dinner?' Molly asks, as she starts placing wine glasses out on the tables.

I don't know what to do with myself? I've never felt awkward like this before. I don't want to stand up the front, speaking down to her from the lectern about dinner. But what else do I do? I'm certainly not going to offer to help. That's too far beneath me. I take the paper and pen I brought and sit down at one of the guest tables, pretending to make notes. The pen is the engraved one that Lachy gave me. I've ended up using it in all my sessions. Despite it being an odd gesture, it's a nice pen, I'll give him that.

'Oh, sorry. You're probably busy preparing,' she says.

I look up and smile at her. 'Dinner was fine, thanks. My steak could probably have used a minute longer on either side but the jus was cooked to perfection.'

'I'll pass that on to Carlos.'

I nod and look back down at my blank page.

Greg returns with water and ice. He unloads ice into some wine coolers and spreads them around the tables. The two of them have just finished setting each table with a red and white wine option and glasses, when the first guests arrive.

'Can you explain the note found in Nadia's room last night?' Tanner asks.

One question.

Only one question about my book before he couldn't help himself.

My cheeks burn and I'm grateful for the dim lighting. I clear my throat. 'No, I can't.' I look at Nadia, who's attempting to hide behind a glass of red wine. 'Nadia, I'm terribly sorry that happened to you.'

She doesn't move. Tanner places a hand on her shoulder. If he thinks that's going to provoke me, he's wrong. I didn't write the damn note.

'How do you explain the initials CM then?' he asks.

This time I address the whole room. 'Raise your hand if you learned to write the alphabet as a child?'

The guests look at each other, faces masked with confusion, but one by one they all raise their hands. Even Tanner.

I smile triumphantly. 'There you go. Everyone in this room has the ability to write my initials.'

Tanner's eyes darken and burn through me. He's clearly not happy I've just humiliated him. This time it's Nadia who comforts Tanner, giving his arm a squeeze.

'Don't you think it's a little odd that just after you told Mr and Mrs Lambert that they should take a break from golf, that their clubs are tampered with?'

I search the room for the voice asking the question. Lachy. What the hell? How is *that* any of his business? He's not even sitting with the Lamberts who, are glaring at him, their faces flushed with embarrassment. I don't think they wanted their dirty laundry aired. What worries me more is that I didn't even know it was their room broken into and I am the person they just spoke to about golf.

Now, there are several people with phones pointed in my direction. *Here we go again.* It's okay. Megan said I need publicity. I need to be relevant again. Maybe people will feel sorry for me or respect the way I answer these idiots.

I offer the Lamberts my kindest smile. 'I'm sorry that this happened to you but I assure you, I had nothing to do with it.'

They nod and return the smile. Mrs Lambert looks as though she's already had plenty of wine, her cheeks a bright pink and her eyes looking glassy.

Then I look to Lachy. 'My conversations with all of you are strictly confidential. Now whether the Lamberts offered you that information or not, it is unfair for you to announce it publicly.'

I let out a big breath and imagine patting myself on the back because *well done me*. I can't believe I didn't lose my cool.

'Are there any questions about *Loveless Marriage*?' I ask, drawing everyone's attention back to my book.

'I have a question.'

It's Andy. The incredibly handsome Andy, only now if looks could kill, I'd be dead. I don't think there's a book question incoming. What could I have possibly done to him? I helped to convince his wife to keep trying for children. I took *his* side.

'Go ahead, Andy.'

'My wife and I haven't told anyone at this retreat about our fertility issues, except you. So, explain to me why Joss found a note attacking her alongside a box of ovulation tests.'

A glass shatters. It's Molly at the back of the room, her mouth hanging open.

'What?' Greg says. 'You didn't report it to us.'

'What's the point?' Andy says. 'You aren't doing anything about these break-ins.'

I'm completely taken by surprise. I feel ambushed. I try to think of the different stalling techniques Megan taught me before I did television or radio interviews and needed a moment to think but my mind is blank.

People keep speaking at me, raising their voices. It all becomes a blur.

The whole room is staring at me. The place is spinning.

I run past the tables, past Molly and out the door.

When I get back to my room, I'm furious. Molly just let them attack me. *She's* the one to blame. This place has non-existent security.

I pace the room. I know what I need to do.

I dial Megan's number and she answers straight away. Probably keen to hear how the Q&A went, and if I got any good content to forward onto her for marketing. She's about to be thoroughly disappointed.

We exchange hellos and I cut to the chase.

'Shit just hit the fan, Megan. Book me a flight home. Preferably tonight, otherwise first thing tomorrow.'

'Whoa, whoa, whoa. Hold on a minute. What's happened?'

I explain the latest turn of events, ending with the angry mob I just ran from.

'I see.'

I can practically hear the wheels turning in her head, trying to work out how to spin this and make it a positive, make it profitable. I'm being accused of leaving threatening notes by people and they claim to have told no one except me about the things the notes reveal. It looks damming and I don't know *how* it's happening. I don't know *how* to spin this.

'Okay,' she finally says. 'I'll come to you. You've signed a contract to host this retreat. You won't get work again if you break it. But I can come there and do damage control. I'll be there early tomorrow.'

'But ...' I begin to protest, before she cuts me off.

'No *buts*, Celia. You can't just leave.'

I want to scream. It's like I'm a prisoner.

'Surely I can say one of the kids is unwell.'

'That'll look like an obvious lie, an easy excuse to run away from whatever's going on there. The public will see right through it.'

I know I'm going to lose this argument. I sigh loudly. 'I hope you have a solid plan by morning.' Then I hang up on her.

Grabbing a bottle of wine, I throw open the front door, ready to find Kitty and get drunk. But as I open the door, Molly is standing there. Her expression is difficult to read. Her eyes are like ice, cold and staring into mine. I can't tell if she's angry or about to burst into tears or both. I also can't tell if her anger is directed at me or if she shares my anger at the psycho mob out there.

'Celia, can we talk?' she asks, her voice shaky and it answers my question—she's trying not to cry.

'I'm on my way out. We'll talk tomorrow when my manager arrives.'

Her shoulders sag. 'Manager?'

'Megan will be here first thing to discuss the rest of the retreat.'

Molly nods slowly. 'Can I get you anything tonight?'

'Have a bottle of Veuve delivered to Kitty's room.' I'm going to need a lot of alcohol tonight. 'And keep that group of psychos away from me,' I say, pointing in the direction of the room we were all in earlier.

'Of course.'

'Oh, and Molly,' I add. 'Cancel my morning therapy sessions. And I'll take breakfast in my room.'

She nods, but says nothing before turning away and rushing back in the direction of the main building.

When I get into Kitty's room, she's halfway through a movie and is completely oblivious to what has happened since dinner.

'Oh wow,' she says, when she sees me. 'You look like shit.'

I glare at her. I don't often lose control but I'm spiralling now. My hair and makeup are surely a mess. I haven't cried, absolutely not. But I have rubbed at my eyes and temples, trying to relieve the pressure and stress building, so I'm sure my makeup is smeared and my hair has flyaways.

Plus, I'm in my pyjamas. A look I never don in public. But the outfit I'd been wearing felt like it was suffocating me almost as much as the barrage of questions were.

Kitty doesn't ask what happened, instead she grabs her phone from the table next to her and begins tapping and scrolling. Her eyes widen more with each passing second.

'How bad is it?' I ask, having not yet had the courage to check social media myself.

'People are accusing you of threatening guests and breaching confidentiality.'

Shit. Not only are they destroying my image but they're risking my reputation as a psychologist. That's my core. That's where I started and what I've always known I can fall back on, if need be. But who's going to trust a psychologist who breaches confidentiality? Even though I absolutely did no such thing.

I pour two very large glasses of wine and sit on the couch next to Kitty.

Handing Kitty a glass and taking a big swig from my own, I fill her in on the evening.

'So after you told an elderly couple to take a break from golf, their clubs were tampered with?' She asks, her brows furrowing.

I nod, trying to read her expression. Is she highlighting the bizarre coincidence or is she actually thinking I could have done this.

'And after the woman reluctantly agreed to keep trying for a baby, which by the way I find totally messed up, she then found a note and a box of ovulation tests?'

'Yes.'

'What the hell, Celia? This is insane.'

My mouth drops open. 'Why are you "what the hell-ing me"? I don't know what's going on.' I try to keep my voice calm but I'm getting increasingly frustrated. Does my best friend honestly think I'm a psychopath? I'm here to regain popularity, not have my name dragged through the mud.

'You're sure no one can access your notes?'

'They're handwritten and my notebook has been with me the whole time.'

She takes a sip of her wine and shakes her head. 'This looks really bad.'

'I know. Megan's on her way.'

Kitty rolls her eyes. 'Good old Megan to the rescue.'

What is that supposed to mean? Is she jealous of Megan and that I went to her first? *Whatever*. Kitty has been far from supportive this entire trip. Why would I go to her?

I hit the play button on the movie Kitty has paused. I have no interest in the movie or in continuing to talk to Kitty but I'm a little nervous to be alone right now, so this will have to do.

Chapter 21

Jocelyn

'Why don't we head to the pool bar?' one of the older, single women suggests.

Celia's Q&A session had taken a dramatic turn when she stormed out but that didn't mean we left. Most of us have finished the bottles of wine provided on our tables but we still aren't ready to call it a night.

Her question is met with a series of yesses before Greg pipes up from the back of the room. 'Sorry, folks. Pool bar's clo—'

Having just returned to the room, Molly cuts him off. 'What a great idea. I'll send someone down to make your drinks.'

Greg narrows his eyes at Molly. I'm guessing that the pool bar opening is an unexpected turn of events. One that Molly probably hopes will win us over after the day of drama.

'Also,' Molly continues, 'unfortunately, the morning's couple therapy sessions are cancelled. We would be more than happy to arrange for some couples massages to replace those session times.'

I steal a glance at Andy, trying to read whether that information is a positive development or not. I know how I feel about it. I have no interest in speaking to Celia and I would kill for a massage right now. Andy's expression doesn't change.

Besides a few of the other guests going back to their rooms, most of us meet at the pool with our swimsuits on and a desire to party. Whatever this retreat has become, we are determined to enjoy it. Perhaps we aren't going to get what we initially came for—a stronger relationship, life advice, a new mindset—but it's Saturday night and we are going to let loose.

Even Andy seems relaxed as he puts an arm around me. 'I love you,' he whispers to me as we sit at the swim-up bar.

'How are you feeling about everything?' I ask.

'We're going to be okay,' he says, leaning across to kiss my shoulder.

I smile, relief and desire flooding through me.

A young girl behind the bar starts making drinks and I wonder if she's been asked to work overtime. A small stab of guilt hits me but we did pay a fortune for this retreat so why shouldn't we have some fun.

Once Andy and I get our drinks, we walk through the water to where a group of other guests are. Some of them are perched on the edge of the pool with their drinks, while others are standing in the water, sipping cocktails from their plastic glasses.

Nadia and Tanner are sitting on the pool edge, talking to one another. His hand is on her thigh and they're looking at each other as though no one else exists in the world. The note hasn't scared them out of whatever *that* is and they aren't even hiding it. I don't think they'd notice if the rest of us disappeared.

Oh well. Good on them. There are no rules to say you can't meet someone here. So what if your goals for being here change, as long as you're happy right?

I ponder that thought. *As long as you're happy*. I will be happy as long as Andy is happy. If that means making some changes to our lifestyle so that we can have children, I'm ready. He went into bat for me tonight. He confronted Celia after what happened and I'm so grateful. That's the kind of man I want to raise my children.

It's after midnight when we finally call it a night and only Tanner and Nadia are left at the pool. We've had far too much to drink and our spirits are high. It's like we're on our honeymoon again. Andy can't stop touching me and we laugh the whole way back to our room.

Outside the door, Andy pulls out the key from his wallet and then stops. He turns to me with the same look he had earlier today. *Twice in one day? And I'm not even ovulating.*

He pulls me into him and our lips meet. Hot, drunken kisses and hands moving all over one another's bodies, which are still dripping wet from the pool.

My insides burn and I want to get him on the other side of that door right now. Andy presses kisses against my neck and I sigh with pleasure. 'Open the door,' I say, my voice breathy.

He swipes the keycard and we stumble in, me pushing him backwards into the room, my hands not leaving his body. Andy's mouth is on mine, even as he fumbles at the wall next to us as he tries to put the keycard in the slot to give the room power.

I giggle and he pulls away from me for a second to see what he's doing. The lights flicker on and I take in the room behind him.

I drop to my knees. Andy turns around to see what I'm reacting to and swears under his breath.

Behind Andy, on our bed is a gift bag. A bright yellow bag with a picture of a bunny on it and the words 'Hello, Baby'. I know as soon as I see it that it came from the intruder. Celia? I don't know. Whoever it is? They're tormenting us again.

Andy helps me to my feet and puts a firm arm around me. Then he opens the bag. There's a box of pregnancy tests on top and I want to vomit at the sight of them. The invasion of privacy, the blatant lack of decency, makes me physically ill. Fertility and conceiving is a personal journey, not a process some outsider can insert themselves into without permission.

Andy places the box of tests on the bed. 'What the hell?' he says, lifting out the next item. It's a tiny white jumpsuit with a yellow duckling print all over it. My eyes fill with tears.

The next item makes Andy yell expletives I've never heard him use before. It's a note.

Nice job earlier. Did it work?

Chapter 22

Molly

I finally get to bed about one am, leaving Greg to clean up the pool bar. I'd sent Lisa home at midnight after she pulled a double shift for me behind the bar. Thankfully, she only lives a few blocks away or I would have made her crash here.

The moment I close my eyes, the phone rings. The line connects to the guest rooms. If they want to continue partying and have food and drink delivered to their rooms, I quit.

'Hello, Molly speaking,' I say, trying to hide any irritation in my voice.

'Hi. It's Andy. There's been another incident. You and Greg need to see this.'

I close my eyes. *Shit*. I wish it had been a call for more booze now.

When I return from Andy and Jocelyn's room, it's time to make the call to my boss. I'd told Joey less than twenty-four hours ago that I had everything under control. I'd texted him earlier tonight saying that I was too busy for him to call but that things were great.

I was wrong. Very wrong.

Not only was the "gift" in their room disgusting and hurtful, the accompanying note was alarming. It inferred that the person leaving the note knew what Jocelyn and Andy were doing behind closed doors, in the privacy of their room. The room I'm charging them for.

I dial Joey's number, grateful that he's in America so that I won't wake him. The reason for this call is probably enough to cost me my job, waking him in the middle of the night would be the cherry on top of his fury.

'Molly,' he says, his voice stern. 'You said you had this under control.'

Surely he can't already know about the latest note. In the background of the call, I hear an announcement.

'My flight is about to board,' he continues. 'I'm on my way back and I'm not happy about ending this trip early.'

'Joey, there's no need to come back.' *Lie.* 'I will handle this.' *Another lie.*

'I'm being sent videos of guests harassing this Celia woman at our resort.'

The Q&A session. Had that been filmed as well? This was way out of my control now.

'There's been a big misunderstanding. Don't worry about it.' I'm not in control of my words either. The lies are just leaving my lips without a second thought and I can't stop them.

'I'll see you as soon as I get in, Molly. Try not to let anything else happen until then.'

He hangs up before I can respond. I blink back tears. *I am so, so fired.*

At seven am, four women from one of the local spas arrive, lugging portable massage tables and a box filled with all sorts of facial creams, body lotions and scented oils. I silently pray that this is enough to keep the couples happy after their therapy sessions were cancelled.

I lead them to two empty rooms and they split up, putting two massage tables in each. I can have two couples being treated at the same time.

I make calls to all of the couples' rooms and let them know where and when their treatment will be and they all sound thrilled. *Win*. I wonder what Joey will think of that.

In the dining room, everything is set for breakfast. I prepare a plate for Celia and take it to her room. When I knock on the door, nobody answers. I try again. Nothing.

I look around, trying to work out what to do. She wanted her food delivered to her room. I can't just leave it on the doorstep. Not for Celia Marsden.

Kitty steps out of her room next door.

'Morning,' I say. 'Is Celia in?'

'She went for a walk on the beach. Is that her breakfast?'

'Yes. She wanted to dine in her room this morning.'

Kitty rolls her eyes and I can't help but wonder how these two women became friends. Kitty seems so down-to-earth. She dines and chats with the other guests and hasn't made a single request or complaint.

'Of course she does,' she says. 'Just leave it on her kitchen bench. She'll be back soon.'

'Thanks.'

'I'm going to go get my breakfast, *with* everyone else.' She smiles and walks away. If Kitty and Celia arrived as best friends, they don't seem to be leaving that way.

I'm nervous to enter Celia's room without her permission. We do room service—deliver food and drink all the time—but there is something different about this situation. It's as though every move we make this weekend could end up a viral video, and not the kind I'd hoped for.

I swipe my master keycard and enter Celia's room. It's a mess. There are several empty wine bottles on the counter and clothes thrown all over the floor. Not what I expected from *Ms Perfect Influencer*. I could photograph this and sell it to the gossip mags and make a killing. That'll help when I'm unemployed. Too bad I have morals. *Stupid conscience.*

I place the tray on the bench and leave. I don't want to be here when Celia returns.

Walking back up to reception, I make a call to Greg and let him know which rooms have the massage therapists in them today, and ask him to get one of the cleaners into Celia's room after breakfast.

A taxi pulls up outside reception just as I arrive. A woman steps out in an emerald-green power suit and strappy peach heels. Her dark hair is pulled back tightly into a high pony-tail, which hangs long down her back and her sunglasses cover most of her face. This must be Megan.

I walk a little faster to meet her at the door.

'Hi, I'm Molly.' I put a hand out to shake hers and she just looks at it.

'Megan,' she confirms, without shaking my hand.

Wow. So she's a clone of Celia. *Excellent.*

The taxi-driver pulls a suitcase from the trunk of the car.

'Be careful with that. It's a Louis Vuitton.' She looks down at the gravel road. 'You'll need to carry it over there.' She points to the reception building where the pavement begins. 'Do not drag it through ...' She scoffs and gestures at the ground. 'This.'

The driver does as instructed and the woman turns to me.

'I'm Celia's manager. Can you show me to her room?'

I'm not sure I can handle two women like this. But I take a deep breath. 'Sure,' I say.

Renowned Psychologist, Celia Marsden, Announces Exclusive Retreat near Byron Bay for Couples and Divorcees

By Kayla Harrison

January 23rd, 2022

In a surprising and exciting turn of events, the celebrated psychologist, author and influential figure in the world of relationships, Celia Marsden, has just unveiled a transformative retreat for couples and recently divorced singles. Marsden, renowned for her groundbreaking book, *Loveless Marriage*, has been relatively quiet on social media recently, leading many to anticipate her next significant endeavour. This retreat, set against the breathtaking backdrop of Byron Bay, promises to be a remarkable opportunity for individuals seeking to rejuvenate their relationships or embark on a fresh journey, post-divorce.

A Haven for Healing and Transformation

Celia Marsden's reputation as a relationship expert precedes her, and her decision to host a retreat of this nature has generated a wave of anticipation among her followers and the general public, alike. With her extensive knowledge and deep understanding of human connections, Marsden is uniquely positioned to guide couples towards rediscovering the love and passion in their relationships.

For those who have recently experienced divorce, the retreat offers a safe space for healing, personal growth and rediscovery. The end of a marriage can be a deeply emotional and challenging time, and Marsden's expertise can provide invaluable support in navigating this transition.

Why Celia Marsden's Retreat is a Game-Changer

Celia Marsden's approach to relationships and her groundbreaking work in her book, *Loveless Marriage*, has resonated with countless individuals seeking answers and solutions to their relationship woes. Her retreat promises to be a game-changer for several reasons:

- **Expert Guidance:** Marsden will personally facilitate workshops and sessions, drawing upon her vast experience as a psychologist to provide attendees with practical tools and insights.

- **Beautiful Location:** Byron Bay, known for its stunning natural beauty and serene ambiance, serves as the perfect backdrop for healing and transformation.

- **Tailored Programs:** The retreat will offer tailored programs for both couples and divorcees, ensuring that participants receive the specific guidance they need.

- **Community and Connection:** Attendees will have the opportunity to connect with others facing similar challenges, fostering a sense of community and support.

- **Holistic Approach:** Marsden's retreat will encompass a holistic approach to well-being, addressing not only emotional and psychological aspects but also physical and spiritual dimensions.

Anticipating High Demand

Given Celia Marsden's influence and reputation, it's expected that spaces for her retreat will fill up quickly but start saving, they're predicted to be a hefty price. Her ability to guide individuals towards healthier, more fulfilling relationships and her compassionate approach to those navigating the complex world of divorce make this retreat a unique and invaluable opportunity. For those seeking to revitalise their relationships or embark on a journey of self-discovery, post-divorce, Marsden's retreat near Byron Bay is an opportunity too good to miss.

Stay tuned for more updates on this exciting news, as Celia Marsden continues to make a positive impact on the world of relationships and personal growth.

Chapter 23

Celia

'I hope you're violently ill right now,' a familiar voice says, as she enters my room.

I get up from the table where I've just eaten breakfast and launch myself into Megan's arms. This is certainly not how we usually greet each other. I rarely hug my loved ones, let alone my manager, but today I feel fragile.

Megan's eyes narrow at the unusual embrace. 'Maybe you are seriously unwell.'

I roll my eyes. 'Why are you so interested in my health right now, when there is so much going on?'

'Your contract says that you will provide everyone on the retreat with two sessions of therapy, either with individuals or with couples.'

I know where she's going with this and I'm not sorry.

Megan continues. 'Unless you are seriously ill right now, you have no excuse to be cancelling sessions.'

'Megs, you didn't see what they were like last night. They were a hungry pack of hyenas and I was a vulnerable little zebra. They destroyed me.'

'You're such a drama queen.' She laughs. 'Where was Kitty when all of this was happening?'

The mention of my so-called best friend makes my blood boil. She's been absolutely no support this entire weekend. 'Who knows,' I snap.

'Well, I'm here now and the first thing we're going to do is get these sessions back up and running.'

My chest tightens. 'No. Absolutely not. You can't possibly expect me to help these people after what they did. Besides, I doubt they even want my help now.'

'Celia, you signed a contract. You need to offer the sessions. If they take you up on the offer, too bad. If they don't, good for you. But if you don't offer them, you'll be forced to give refunds and the repercussions of that to your image would come at an even higher cost.'

I sigh. She's right. But I can't bear the thought of facing them. These people think I've been breaking into their rooms, threatening them. It's insane.

'Look, we can probably cancel the book reading,' she adds, trying to persuade me.

Shit. I'd almost forgotten about the stupid book reading event where I'm expected to read excerpts of my book aloud for the guests. 'Fine,' I say.

With some expert reorganising by Megan, I'm able to meet with the couples who are still keen to see me and work around their massages. By cutting most of my lunch break and cancelling the book reading, we make it work. It helps that three of the couples were not interested in having a session today. *Suits me.*

During the ten minutes Megan has scheduled for me to have lunch, she joins me in my room to eat. I pick at some strips of grilled chicken that make up my Caesar salad.

'Okay,' she says, game face on.

When Megan is concocting a plan, her face changes. I tease her and call it her game face. Her eyebrows pinch in the middle and I warn her about the wrinkles she's creating. Her mouth forms a straight line and her eyes narrow. It's always a warning sign for me that something big is in the works.

'We need to spin all the drama from this weekend into a positive. People need to read about this retreat and feel like they want to come if there's a next time or we want them to feel sorry for you.'

I almost choke on a crouton. 'Hold it right there. There's absolutely no way that there'll be another retreat. This is the first and absolutely last of its kind.'

'This retreat has already brought in a lot of money,' she counters. 'And the publicity is priceless.'

'The publicity is career-destroying. I'm being accused of breaking and entering, and of leaking confidential information'

'Well, lucky you have me,' she says, and winks. 'I have the perfect plan.'

Chapter 24

Nadia

The last two days have been life-changing. I'm sure that's the sort of review Celia would hope for when people ask me about how the retreat was. However, it is in spite of Celia that it has been life-changing.

I have found my confidence again. The Nadia of the past two years would never have stuck up for herself the way I did with Celia. I would have shied away from any sort of conflict. The divorced Nadia didn't socialise, she hid away, abusing alcohol and sending her parents crazy. And here I am making friends, making *more* than friends.

I'm not really sure where I stand with Tanner. He stood up for me last night and we had another fun evening getting to know each other. But then he gave me a peck on the lips and wished me goodnight despite me dropping constant hints about being interested in taking it further. Not only was I enjoying his company but I had needs that hadn't revealed themselves lately but were now screaming at me to fulfil them. Strong, attractive, kind Tanner was what I needed.

Celia's manager called this morning to ask if I still wanted to have my therapy session. I didn't go yesterday but I've paid for them so I said I'd be there. I need to do one, for Mum and Dad's sake. Plus Tanner had said going would surprise her and maybe she'll make a mistake. Walking over to the recreation room now, I'm glad I agreed to it. I'm ready to put all of the Celia drama behind me. I don't care what she thinks but I do want to speak to her. Isn't that part of me finding myself? Being able to put conflict behind me and rise above?

I open the door, feeling relaxed and confident but my breath hitches when I see Celia sitting in an armchair. Last time we all saw her, we'd basically spooked her into running back to her room. And now, she looks pissed. Her arms are crossed and her eyes don't meet mine. She says nothing as I sit opposite her, her mouth firm in a straight line.

'Hi,' I say, my cool, calm and collected vibe leaking from my body at a rapid rate.

'I'm surprised you came,' she says, her voice icy.

'Well, I missed my session yesterday—'

'Because you thought I'd broken into your room,' she snaps, cutting me off. 'What's changed today?'

It was a fair question. And to be honest, nothing had changed. All the evidence still points to her and with the additional break ins, it was hard to see how someone else could've known the information and done it.

I take a deep breath. 'Nothing has really changed. But I did want to say that this weekend has helped me in other ways and I'm grateful that I could be a part of it.'

'So you're here to brag that you're leaving the retreat a happier person, despite not utilising my services?'

'Umm.' *Oops.* I'm not bragging. I'm just trying to leave on good terms. Or better terms. This isn't going well.

'You yelled at me at breakfast yesterday and that went viral on social media. Then your boyfriend yelled at me last night. So, why are you here?'

'Tanner is not my boyfriend,' I say, ignoring her question.

'Whatever you two are, I don't care. You both ignored my advice to focus on yourselves as singles. Then you accuse me of threatening you.

You verbally attack me. And now you're here to say *thanks for having me.*'

I squeeze the arms of the chair. I'm officially all out of confidence.

She continues. 'You are most certainly not welcome. And you will be hearing from my lawyer when this trip is over. Nobody defames my name and gets away with it.'

I sit there for a moment, unsure if she's finished scolding me or if I can leave. She clears her throat and when she says nothing, I rush outside. Inside the rec room, I'd felt so small and intimidated but as I walk further away from Celia Marsden, the anger builds.

Whether she left the note or not, I'm a paying customer on her retreat. There's no excuse for someone breaking into my room and leaving threats. She hasn't once asked if I'm okay after the break-in. If she's so innocent, maybe she should have done that.

Twitter Excerpt

Tweet from @CeliaMarsdenTherapy

August 15th, 2021

Happy birthday to my bestie @KittyAnhPsych You've seen the best and worst of me and still stick by my side. Love you Kitty Kat

Comments:

@KittyAnhPsych Thanks hun. Boy do I have some stories I could sell but I still love you

@CeliaMarsdenTherapy: @KittyAnhPsych you wouldn't!

@Chelsealoves: @KittyAnhPsych tell us more! Tell us more!

@KittyAnhPsych: @Chelsealoves Sorry! What happens at uni, stays at uni. Right @CeliaMarsdenTherapy?

@Chelsealoves: awww that's so sweet you're still besties from your young days

Chapter 25

Celia

My final therapy sessions with the guests were painful. Each word they uttered was like nails scraping down a blackboard. Each moment that ticked by sucked more patience and more energy from me so that by the time I finished, I felt like a shadow of my true self. A skeleton. Nothing left to give.

But I am required to attend dinner. Megan was quick to remind me. It's all part of her elaborate publicity plan so I have no choice.

'Knock, knock,' Kitty's sing-song voice calls from the front door of my room.

I drop my head back and sigh. I can't deal with her right now. The hum of the shower running filters through the closed bathroom door and I try to mentally will Megan to make it quick so I'm not left alone with Kitty too long. Molly gave Megan one of the standard rooms, which she is happy to sleep in, but I told her she could use my ensuite after she told me that the decor in her bathroom included yellowing tiles and a suspicious stain on the ceiling.

'Celia, unlock the door,' Kitty calls, her voice no longer chirpy.

My Louboutin heels clack along the tiled flooring and I open the door for Kitty.

She walks past me, not even taking in the glare I direct at her, and makes herself comfortable on a stool at the bench. I follow her into the kitchen and living space and stand on the other side of the bench opposite her.

'Barely seen you today,' I say, my voice like ice. I hope she realises that it's an accusation. I can't believe she has joined me on this trip only to abuse the friendship by enjoying every available luxury but not offering an ounce of support. I thought that was a pretty clear, albeit unwritten, rule of this arrangement.

'Well yeah because you didn't come to breakfast this morning and you hid in here with Megan when you weren't working.'

I narrow my eyes at her. 'Why the hell would I go to breakfast after what they did to me last night?' My palms are flat on the bench and I press them harder into the cold surface, hoping to relieve the anger quickly building inside me.

'Because it's your job.'

'My job?' I slap one of my hands hard on the benchtop and the stinging sensation lingers far longer than I expect.

'You are here to help people. Well, that's what you claim. That's what your book claims. Or are you just here to get more followers? Get more sales?'

My cheeks burn. 'How dare you?'

'What? Call you out on it finally? There are people here who have been threatened, had confidential information disclosed and you are playing the victim.'

I can barely hear her speaking now. My anger is bubbling in my ears, a ringing noise making my head pound. I lean my elbows on the bench and drop my head in my hands, massaging my temples with my index fingers.

Kitty has been my best friend for such a long time. I don't understand how she can turn on me like this. Is it years of jealousy built up inside of her and now she's finally cracking? We graduated together but after a few years my career took off, powered down another path, and I went from living in relative comfort to living in luxury. Is that what this is about?

I lift my head, staring her in the eyes. 'You've always been jealous.'

She laughs. She actually laughs. 'You know what, Celia. I may not have designer clothing or a fancy house but I have my dignity. I can say without a doubt that I put my patients first. Can you?'

'Get out!' I yell.

Our heated conversation had drowned out the sound of the shower. It must've stopped while we were arguing and Megan emerges from the bathroom in a robe, her hair dripping wet. Her eyes are wide as she looks between us. Both Kitty and I sharing the same red-cheeked, furious expressions.

'What's going on?' she asks. 'Celia, there are guests in earshot don't forget. This is terrible—'

Kitty cuts her off. 'Publicity?' She rolls her eyes. 'Don't worry, I was just leaving.'

Kitty slams the door behind her. Off she goes to her room, paid for by me. *Good luck getting home. You're on your own now.*

'What was that all about?' Megan asks, as she towel dries her hair.

I shake my head. 'It's nothing.' I take a new bottle of Veuve from the fridge and hand it to Megan. 'Do you mind?'

'I'm not your bloody maid,' she says, but obliges anyway, opening the bottle with a sweet pop. 'And it didn't sound like nothing.'

I take the bottle from her and pour us both a large glass.

'Celia, we have a plan now. Don't make this worse.'

I take a large swig of the bubbly liquid and smile. 'Just go get ready will you? If you're going to make me go to dinner, you're coming too.'

Twenty minutes later, Megan and I walk in the direction of the dining room. I've had half of the bottle of Veuve now and it has done nothing to ease the tension consuming me. I don't care what these guests think of me anymore. I know I've done nothing wrong. But I don't relish the thought of dining with a room full of people who think I've been threatening them and sharing private information about them.

My long designer kaftan whips wildly around my legs. We've had perfect weather for this retreat but tonight is cooler, the ocean sounds angry, and I have the sensation of imminent doom. Not that I need a sensation to tell me that doom is imminent. It is rather obvious. However, the sensation is there and it's making the bubbles of the champagne burn my insides.

When we enter the dining room, it falls silent. They were clearly talking about us. Well, me. Probably discussing whether I'd actually come to dinner. I wish I wasn't here and steal a look at Megan, cursing her internally for making me do this. She looks totally unphased by the situation, rocking white tailored pants, a hot pink silk shirt and matching heels. Megan always looks like she's in control. Her head could be swarming with information, with stress, and no one would know. But I suppose a powerful looking publicist is necessary. I just hope I'm faking it as well as she is.

I plant a smile on my face as Megan and I take a seat at an empty table.

Molly rushes over, one hand holding a bottle of red wine and the other a bottle of white.

'So pleased you could join us tonight, Ms Marsden.' Then she looks at Megan. 'And Megan of course. Red or white wine this evening?'

I give her a look of disapproval. How can I possibly make that decision if I don't know what we're eating tonight.

'Something wrong?' she asks.

'What's being served tonight?'

She smiles. 'Carlos has prepared smoked duck breast with chestnut gnocchi and kale. He recommends the pinot noir with his dish.' She holds up the bottle of red.

'Red it is then,' I say.

Megan and I don't say much before dinner, just sip our wines. The whole room is tense. There is an occasional low murmuring of chatter but mostly it's an eerie silence. People glance at me and then quickly look away when our eyes meet. Guests lean into one another and whisper things, before looking in my direction. The whole situation is humiliating. I feel like a child at school who has just been destroyed by a bully in front of the whole cafeteria. Now, no one wants to speak to me or sit with me, they just want to talk about me. If only I could take my dinner and eat it in the bathroom cubicle like they do in the movies.

The duck is brought out, myself and Megan served first. I've got to give it to Carlos. It looks and smells incredible. My mouth literally salivating, I lift my fork to my lips. I bite into the juicy meat, closing my eyes and savouring a small positive from this evening.

When I open my eyes, the entire room is staring at me. As I swallow that first mouthful, they all turn back to one another, one table exchanging five dollar notes. My eyes narrow. What the hell was that about?

'What?' I snap, as Molly continues to place plates down in front of the other diners.

No one responds.

I stand and walk over to the table that had been passing money around. Of course, Nadia and Tanner are sitting here, along with Lachy, Jocelyn and Andy; smug looks on their faces.

'What was that about?'

Nadia sniggers. She's clearly past her moment of gratitude toward me and this retreat. I glare at her and she suppresses a smile.

'Oh, screw it,' Jocelyn says. 'We placed bets to see if you'd actually eat your meal tonight without complaining or sending it back.'

My mouth hangs open for a moment before I compose myself.

'What a coincidence? I was just placing a bet on whether your relationship would last. The odds are slim.'

Then I storm out of the dining room, the sound of Megan's pink heels trotting after me.

When I get outside, the wind is even stronger than before and the ground is wet from earlier rain.

'Celia, that duck is divine. Are you really storming out?'

'I'm not putting up with that. Molly will bring our food to my room.'

'Are we sticking to the plan?' she asks.

I nod and then wrap my arms around myself to protect myself from the cold.

Chapter 26

Nadia

I'm still giggling when the clacking of Celia and Megan's heels fade into the distance and then stops all together, as the door closes behind them. When did this retreat turn into a bitchy school camp? Yes, we've had a few wines and made that silly bet but then Celia's comeback was just pathetic. Exactly how I imagine a teenager would retort before slamming their bedroom door behind them.

I'm not disappointed that she's gone though. The whole room felt tense with her here. Even the couples and singles who hadn't had a run in with her during their sessions or via a creepy break-and-enter were now sick to death of her. It is basically a silent agreement now that this evening, our last night, is about having a good time and forgetting about the tornado that is Celia Marsden.

Just as the mutual sigh of relief around the room settles, Kitty walks in. *Great.* She's probably been sent for damage control or to collect something for Queen Celia.

'Celia's not here,' Jocelyn says, calling to her from our table.

Kitty turns to her and smiles, a mischievous glint in her eyes. 'Good.' Then she pulls a chair over to our table and sits down next to me.

Molly begins fussing around her, setting up cutlery and placing a fresh wine glass in front of her.

'It's okay,' Kitty says. 'I know I'm late. I understand if I've missed dinner.'

Molly holds up the two wine bottles and Kitty points to the white.

'Don't be silly. You're a guest, dinner will just be a few minutes,' Molly responds, her voice panicked.

Kitty places a hand on Molly's shaking wrist as she begins to pour her wine.

'Really, it's fine. I'm not like *her*.'

The way she says "her" is with so much venom that I immediately know she's talking about Celia. Interesting. It would seem the queen has lost her loyal follower.

Molly doesn't acknowledge Kitty's comment, instead just rushes away, bottles in hand.

Jocelyn, who I've discovered loves to gossip and doesn't shy away from drama, is first to ask what we're all thinking.

'What happened with Celia?' Jocelyn's eyes are practically bulging out of her head, staring at Kitty with such intensity as if what she has to say could be the answer to world peace.

Kitty sighs. 'We had an argument.'

'About?' Jocelyn asks, and Andy gives her a glare that suggests she mind her own business.

'I said some things I should have said years ago.' She takes a drink from her wine glass, swallowing almost half of its contents. 'She used to be a psychologist who wanted to help people, help couples. But then that bloody book happened.'

Shit. The book. I'd almost forgotten about it. I wonder if Mum will still want her freshly signed copy once I tell her what Celia's really like.

Kitty continues. 'She became more interested in fame and followers after that. Your sessions with her are the first therapy sessions she's done in years. I don't know how she's managed to maintain her registration as a psychologist.'

Everyone around the table just stares at her. Joss looks like a kid at Disneyland while Andy sits next to her shaking his head. Lachy's face is difficult to read. I don't know him well but usually he is an open book, never shuts up. Tanner is angry. I can tell from the way his neck is burning red and his eyes are narrowed in a way that would make me scared to be in his firing line.

'You mean she's charged us for this retreat and she's not even a practising psychologist?' Tanner asks.

'Nope,' Kitty says, and takes another gulp of wine. 'Not recently anyway.' There is definitely no love lost there.

'Where is she now?' Lachy finally speaks.

Kitty looks at him like a woman who has just been asked her age. 'Uh, I don't know. Not here. That's all I care about.'

Lachy excuses himself and then leaves. It's odd, but not really for Lachy. He is odd. Jocelyn had said that he got weirdly aggressive with her at the pool earlier and then acted like nothing happened when he saw her later. Who knows what's going through his head.

Tanner and I sit with Kitty, Jocelyn and Andy awhile longer, enjoying more wine as well as a tiramisu that puts my mum's recipe to absolute shame—not that I'd ever tell her that. Kitty and Jocelyn spend most of the time nattering about Celia or other influencers that I don't know much about. When I hid away from most of the world these past months, that included the social media world too. My mum clocks more hours on any of those platforms than I do.

'Let's get out of here,' I whisper to Tanner.

I still had those needs that hadn't been met yet and they were burning hotter each passing moment I was with him.

He smiles. 'Gladly.'

We leave the dining room and head towards the beach. A storm had passed through during dinner. Now the only evidence of it was a few puddles on the footpaths and the welcome drop in temperature.

We remove our shoes and step on to the cold, damp sand. I tip my head back and let the ocean breeze whip my hair back. I shiver. It had been much warmer when I'd gotten dressed for dinner and my mini skirt and singlet top were doing nothing to keep me warm now.

Tanner wraps a strong arm around me and rubs at the skin on my arms, trying and failing to dissuade the goosebumps from prickling at my skin. I move in closer to him so that my cheek is pressed against his chest and he embraces me, both arms wrapped around me now and I stop shivering.

'This retreat has been insane,' he whispers in my ear, barely loud enough to hear over the crashing waves. The storm may be over but the waves are still angry, large white horses rushing at speed in our direction before violently falling and washing away. 'But I'm so glad I'm here.'

I lift my head to look at him. 'Me too.'

'I didn't come here looking for anything like this,' he says, his eyes boring into mine. 'But I feel like this is why we were meant to be here.'

I nod and my stomach is alive with butterflies. Tanner has opened up to me about his life a lot this weekend but I don't know what he thinks of whatever *this* is.

'You'll visit me in Brisbane, yeah?' he asks.

Brisbane is only an hour drive from the Gold Coast, an option I don't have considering I don't have a licence. But there are buses and trains and hell, I've got nothing keeping me on the Gold Coast anyway right now, except a room in Mum and Dad's house—the same room I occupied as a child. Although maybe I'm getting ahead of myself.

'Definitely,' I reply, trying not to sound as though I'd been mentally planning to move my life to another city for him.

He tucks a windswept strand of hair behind my ear, only for it to be whipped away again and we both laugh. He rests his hand below my ear on the side of my neck and I lean my head into it.

'I don't want this to end, Nadia. I want to make this work.'

My entire body feels like jelly. This feeling is new. I thought my ex was the dreamiest man I'd ever met. I fell hard and fast. But he never opened up to me. We didn't have long meaningful conversations.

This feeling is new because I've never felt so close to a man. I've never felt comfortable enough to share my emotions in this way. Tanner makes me feel safe and he's already shown me that he'll have my back and protect me. It's been three days but maybe this is what they're talking about when people say, "it was love at first sight".

A tear runs down my cheek and he wipes it away gently with his thumb.

'Are you okay?' he asks.

I nod. 'Yes. I want to make this work too.'

Then he leans down and kisses me. A gentle, passionate kiss that lasts a long time but not long enough. My hands grip at the front of his shirt and his explore my back, waist and down to the hem of my short skirt. My breath catches and I lift to my toes, pulling him closer and bringing a leg up to his side so that my skirt hitches up. He takes my lead and runs a hand down my thigh and then back up, his fingers sliding underneath the hem.

I press my body even harder against his, every part of me wanting to get as close as possible to him. His hand moves further up and I pull my lips away, dropping my head back and breathing heavily as the sea breeze washes over my face. Then he begins kissing my neck, warm and soft and I sigh. I need more.

I feel his own response pressed against the front of my skirt and I can't take it anymore.

'Let's go back,' I say, breathless.

He moans against my neck in agreement and then pulls away from me. He gives me one last peck on the lips before we head back up to the resort.

When my room is in sight, I realise I don't have my key with me. It's in my bag, which is still sitting under the table in the dining room.

'Shit,' I mutter. 'I'll meet you at your room.'

Then he kisses me again, just quickly but with a teasing flick of his tongue. 'Don't be long.'

Chapter 27

Jocelyn

What a night! I am sufficiently plastered, thanks to a few too many glasses of wine with Kitty and Andy. The three of us were egging each other on like teenagers. At one point, we even asked for shots, to which Molly replied that they were not that sort of establishment.

It didn't matter though, the wine was enough. Andy was actually joining in on the conversation about Celia even when we were talking about influencers and social media. Who would've thought. Although if he hadn't joined in, he'd literally have been sitting on his own since Lachy, Tanner and Nadia had made pretty early exits.

'Sorry,' Molly says. She looks exhausted. Her hair is tied back but there are flyaways everywhere and her clothes are covered in smears of food and splashes of red wine. 'We're about to close the bar.'

I glance around the dining room. We are the last ones here.

'One more round,' I say, and I swear there is a flash of annoyance in Molly's eyes before she smiles and walks over to the bar.

'I still can't believe this weekend,' I say, giggling as I sip my wine. 'Andy, I'm sorry this isn't what you signed up for.'

He shrugs and his eyes are glassy. 'No, but at least we've had some fun tonight. Like the old days.'

We clink our glasses and Kitty joins in too, not that she knows anything about our relationship because we've only discussed the really hard-hitting issues this evening, such as Celia's Instagram page, and influencers who pretend to use products in ads for money but don't actually use them. We'd laughed uncontrollably for five minutes at a video of a reality TV star, pretending to rub some miracle moisturiser into her face but not realising she hadn't taken the lid off. The comments were hilarious.

'To Celia's fucked up retreat,' Andy says, and we clink our glasses again.

'To fake psychologists and shitty best friends,' Kitty adds. Another clink and now we're laughing.

'To threatening notes and ovulation tests,' I say, lifting my glass.

But there's no clink.

'Too soon?' I ask sheepishly.

Andy's face softens.

'I heard about that,' Kitty says. 'That is beyond disgusting, what happened to you, and I hope you find out who did it.'

I shrug. 'Whatever. We'll be home tomorrow.' Even though, deep down, I still feel really sick about it—the thought of someone knowing about our history and then knowing we'd just had sex.

I take the last sip of my wine and Nadia comes rushing in. Her hair is dishevelled, shoes in her hands and her feet covered in sand.

'Are you okay?' I ask.

'Yeah,' she says, and as she gets closer I spy the unmistakable redness of a pash rash on her cheek and neck. 'Just forgot my bag.' She ducks down beneath the table. 'Got it. Night.'

'Have fun,' I say, giving her a wink and she smiles.

'I will.'

Chapter 28

Nadia

I go back to my own room before Tanner's to freshen up a bit. I'm sandy and my hair is knotted from the wind on the beach. Now that I have my bag back, I check my phone. Several messages and missed calls from my mum:

There are more stories online about the retreat. Are you okay?

Nadia, answer me. Are you okay?

If I don't hear from you in the next hour, I'm calling the police.

Oh for crying out loud, Mum. I check the time of her last message. She only sent it a moment ago. I quickly call her before she sends the police into a frenzy over nothing.

'Nadia, darling. Where have you been?' Mum's voice is frantic and her accent is thicker when she's like this.

'Relax. I just left my phone in another room.'

'What room? Whose room? What is going on?' I can picture her Italian hand gestures as she barks at me down the phone.

'The dining room. Mum, I'm fine. I'm actually having a nice time.'

'Nice time!' she yells. 'This retreat looks like a disaster online. It is not a nice time.'

I sigh. I'm not going to tell her I've met someone when she's like this. 'Mum, I'll see you tomorrow. Pick up is ten am.'

'Oh Nadia, you will give your father and I a heart attack. Keep your phone near you. Ciao.'

I shake my head as I hit the red hang-up button and remind myself that she means well even if it does feel like she's smothering me sometimes.

I grab my handbag and phone charger, heaven forbid my phone dies while I'm with Tanner, and lock my room door behind me, having put the lamp back in place. He's probably wondering where I am by now.

When I get to his room, the door is unlocked and I let myself in. He looks up and smiles. A bottle of wine and two glasses sit on the bedside table.

'Wine?' he asks and I nod. 'Where did you get to?'

'Sorry, my mum was freaking out because I didn't reply to her messages. Just giving her proof of life before I got here.'

He laughs and hands me a glass.

'Cheers,' he says. 'To us. I'm so glad our divorces brought us here.'

This time we both laugh and take a sip. Then he takes my glass from my hand and puts it with his back on the table. He steps closer to me and I breathe him in—cologne combined with salty air and wine on his breath.

'Now,' he says, his voice suddenly husky. 'Where were we?'

I move towards him. Our bodies are only an inch apart. I go to speak and he places a finger on my lips, then traces down my neck, my collarbone. My skin tingles where he's touched it. He continues down, his hand sliding down one of the thin straps of my top. He doesn't take his eyes off me the entire time and it takes all my willpower to not push him onto the bed behind him and jump on top.

His hand reaches my breast and he brushes his thumb over my bare nipple. I shudder and then he leans in. This time there's no gentle kiss first. It's hard and hot and I press myself against him. One of his hands is at my breast as the other slips the other strap down. He pulls away from my lips and moves down so that his tongue is flicking my nipple and I cry out. It has been so long since a man touched me.

Tanner continues planting kisses down my stomach, unzipping the back of my mini skirt at the same time. He pushes my skirt to the floor and then turns us around so that now the bed is behind me. He lies me down, my legs still hanging over the edge of the bed. Then he kneels down between them.

Ripping my underwear away in one fast movement, my back arches the first time his mouth touches me, and I worry I may be finished before I even get a second to savour it. Tanner moves his tongue and I grip the bed either side of me.

'Holy shit,' I say, as his tongue moves faster and I feel myself climaxing.

Then he adds a finger and I'm gone. The pleasure is too much and his name is on my every breath as I reach that moment and the room explodes around me.

Tanner joins me on the bed. I'm still breathless as he begins kissing me.

I whisper. 'I want more.'

He sighs against my lips. 'You sure?'

'Yes. Please, Tanner.' My words come out more desperate than I intended.

He makes fast work of a condom he has on the bedside table. I hadn't even noticed it before. Then he pauses, his tip just outside me and I try to push up to meet him.

'Come on,' I say, putting my hand around his neck and pulling his lips to mine.

He pushes himself inside me and moans. He feels so good filling me and I push my hips closer to him, trying to take every last bit of him.

Then he moves and I lose myself.

I lie in bed next to Tanner in a state of pleasure and a buzz of anticipation of what *this* may be. There is definitely a spark. More than a spark. An explosion.

But since that moment of climax, he hasn't said a word and my anxiety is through the roof. I haven't been with anyone since my ex and perhaps I wasn't doing it properly or the way Tanner likes it. Maybe, I was too fast. Why isn't he speaking?

'Everything okay?' I ask, drawing circles on his bare chest with my finger.

He clears his throat. 'Yeah of course.'

'You've been really quiet, that's all. Was I okay?' Ugh. I hate myself for asking. It's so needy. I'm sure Tanner isn't interested in lying here and stroking my ego, convincing me that the sex was okay.

'Better than okay.' He smiles and pecks me on the lips. 'I'm going for a walk.'

I sit up. 'Now? It's so late.'

'Yeah. I just need some fresh air.' He throws on his clothes. 'I'll be back soon.'

Then he leaves and I'm left sitting in the bed feeling rejected and like a complete fool. It's midnight and he's taking a walk. If he's got so much energy, why isn't he gearing up for round two? Because round one was such a bitter disappointment?

I close my eyes, although I'm certain sleep won't come.

Chapter 29

Jocelyn

I can't sleep. Andy snores next to me, in a wine-induced coma but I'm too riled up.

I had said "whatever" to Kitty as though the weekend's events hadn't rattled me but now that the buzz of the wine has worn off, I'm furious. Still no one has been held responsible for our two break-ins and notes. Not to mention the fact that one of the notes infers that they were watching us or listening to us. Ugh. It's creepy. Disgusting. It makes my skin crawl just thinking about it. And are they still listening now?

All signs point to Celia. Her initials. Her knowing our fertility issues. And who knows? She probably has lackeys everywhere checking in on all her "clients".

That's another thing. How can she charge us for a retreat that includes therapy sessions, when she hasn't practised psychology in years? The whole thing reeks of a scam, a set up.

I toss and turn, getting increasingly frustrated and angry. I tap my phone to check the time.

After midnight.

Screw it.

I don't care how late it is. I'm going to confront her one last time.

I throw a jumper on over my silk pyjamas and slip my Birkenstocks on. Then I march over to Celia's room. Her room is on the other side of the pool nearer to the beach. I approach her front door and a wave of nerves washes over me because I don't exactly know what I'm going to say. I'm about to knock when there's a loud pop, like the top coming off a bottle of champagne. It comes from the back of Celia's room. She must be on her balcony. *Good. She's awake.*

I round the side of the room until the balcony is in view. Celia is drinking straight from a bottle of Veuve and pacing her balcony, muttering who knows what to herself. Classy.

I take a few steps back before she can see me and then dart from the side of the room to the shrubs a few metres away. I crouch down, watching her. It's like a car wreck. Disturbing to watch but I can't look away.

Then I get an idea. Leverage.

An influencer as sophisticated and intelligent as Celia Marsden would never want to be caught getting drunk and talking to herself on her balcony. What better way to make her come clean about the notes and reimburse us for this shit show of a trip than with a little blackmail.

I take out my phone and start snapping. I even record a short video, where it's clear she is chirping away to herself. *Gotcha.*

Suddenly, Celia stops pacing and looks inside. Something has gotten her attention but most of the lights are off inside so I can't see much, just a coffee table in front of a sofa just beyond the back door.

Celia steps inside.

There's a cracking sound to my right. The sound of a stick breaking under someone's foot. But it has been a windy night, there are probably branches cracking all over the place. I can't see anything, just more thick green shrubbery and beyond it in the distance, the beach. I take a deep breath and turn back to the room. Celia is standing there looking right in my direction. I gasp and quickly cover my mouth. There is no way she can see me. I'm deep in the bushes under the cover of night.

She's not moving. Just swaying on the spot, bottle of Veuve in a hand hanging by her side.

I should just go and talk to her now. I've got the photos and videos to threaten her. Let's get it done. Rip it off like a Band-Aid.

I'm just about to creep out of my hiding place when a figure approaches Celia from behind. I can't see who it is, their face blanketed in darkness. I freeze on the spot.

Celia doesn't seem to register that they're even there. She takes another swig from her bottle.

Then the figure behind reaches out and pushes Celia hard in the back. She lurches forward with such force that her head flings back as her body falls. Just before she hits the ground, her head slams into the corner of the coffee table and the bottle of Veuve rolls out of her hand.

My heart races. What the hell have I just witnessed? The figure disappears, retreating further back into the room, away from the balcony window.

I crouch there in the bushes, completely frozen.

Is she dead? Did someone just kill Celia Marsden?

Her body hasn't moved since she fell. I have to go help her.

But what if the attacker is still inside? Or what if someone thinks I did it? Everyone heard me talking about her at dinner. Plus the photos in my phone. I could delete them but I'm sure they stay permanently somewhere in the cloud.

No. I can't go in there. It's too risky.

Another cracking sound pierces the night air. Then footsteps. The unmistakable sound of footsteps moving and moving quickly.

I have to get back. It's not safe out here.

But there's another noise to my right. I squint through the darkness, trying to see any kind of movement through the bushes. It's not the attacker because their footsteps led away from here. Was someone else out here with me? Did someone else just witness what I saw? I hold my breath and stand as still as possible. I watch as minutes tick over on my smartwatch. Three minutes and not a sound. It must be the wind.

I creep through the bushes until I'm out on the footpath but not so close to Celia's room any more. I don't want to be spotted near the scene of the crime and I don't want to be anywhere near her attacker.

I make it back to my room and lock the door behind me, my chest heaving and I try to take in air. The adrenaline courses through my veins as I try to process what just happened.

'Joss?' Andy says, rolling over. 'That you?'

'Yep. Go back to sleep. I'm just using the bathroom.'

Then I sit on the bathroom floor, hug my knees into my chest and cry.

Chapter 30

Molly

This retreat has been a disaster. I'll almost certainly lose my job and no doubt both Sand & Salt's and my reputation will be blasted all over social media by Celia Marsden.

I will struggle to find somewhere else to work because I'll forever be associated with all these viral videos of Celia being trolled by guests of the resort I was managing. With this region being all about influencers and celebrities these days, nobody is going to want to be hosted by yours truly. Introducing Molly—unemployed, middle-aged loser. You'll find me at my parents' place.

'Greg,' I call from the desk in the reception area. He's in the laundry room next door helping me out with the tablecloths and napkins from last night's dinner. I was not expecting it to be a red wine induced farewell party and my white napery has seen better days.

Greg pokes his head around the doorframe. 'Yep?'

'I'm headed over to Celia's room to see if she's having breakfast there again.'

'You got it, boss. Final meal for the queen.'

I shake my head. How can he still be making jokes? His job is on the line too.

Making my way over to Celia's room, I run through the worst case scenarios in my head. By the time I get to her door, I've basically calculated my welfare payments for the next month.

I knock on her door but she doesn't respond. The light is on inside but no movement. I walk around to the balcony at the back in case she's enjoying her last morning overlooking the ocean but she's not outside.

As I approach the back door, Kitty steps out onto her balcony in the next room over.

'Morning,' she says, stretching her arms over her head and taking in the view. If only Kitty had as much public reach as her bestie because she seems to have had a great time.

'Morning. Have you seen Celia today?'

Her relaxed expression changes and her eyes narrow. 'No. In fact, can you possibly help me with changing my flight home? I don't want to be stuck next to her on a plane.'

I try to keep my face neutral. I guess she hasn't had a perfect time after all. Could there be any more drama?

'Of course,' I say, 'I'll get someone to help you with that this morning.'

She smiles before returning to her room.

I'm about to knock on the glass sliding door, when I see a figure on the floor just inside.

What the hell? Is that a body?

The door is unlocked and I slide it open. Celia is lying face down next to the coffee table. Blood staining the rug underneath her.

'Celia,' I kneel down, placing a hand on her back. 'Celia, can you hear me?' I give her a gentle shake.

Nothing.

I push her so that she rolls on to her back.

Nothing.

She lies there motionless, a deep cut on her forehead, which I'm thankful to see isn't still bleeding.

I give her one last shake, shouting her name loudly.

She makes a gurgling moaning sound and I sigh with relief. She's not dead. Talk about worst case scenarios. That would have taken the cake.

I shoot off a text to Greg and then call an ambulance.

The ambulance arrives along with a police car. By the time the paramedics are loading Celia into the ambulance, she has come to and is babbling about an attack.

Surely not. A bottle of champagne lay at her side and there was another empty bottle on the kitchen counter. She was drunk and fell. Now, she's embarrassed and doesn't want to ruin her perfect influencer image.

However, the police are taking her seriously and her manager is shouting all kinds of legal threats as she climbs into the ambulance with Celia.

Kitty is a mess, begging the paramedics to allow her to go too. I suppose she's over their little tiff. Events like this do have that effect sometimes. The paramedic explains, again, that only one person can ride in the ambulance and that she can meet them at the hospital. This just makes Kitty sob louder. A police woman puts a comforting arm around her and says that she'd be happy to take Kitty to the hospital in a few hours.

A few hours?

No. These guests are to be checked out by 10am. That's forty-five minutes away and I don't intend to put one extra minute into these people who have ruined my life. I don't care what happened, they need to leave.

I run my hands through my hair and catch a glimpse of my reflection in the window of Celia's room. Who the hell am I? What have I become? A woman has been seriously hurt and I'm worried about working longer. I pride myself on my hospitality but I'm struggling. I squeeze my eyes closed and all I can see is Celia's head and a pool of blood.

A gentle hand rubs my back. 'Molly, mate, are you okay?'

I look up at Greg and the waterworks flow.

'Oh Mol, come here.' He pulls me in for a hug. 'This is bloody messed up. You wouldn't read about it.'

He rubs my back and the tears slow.

'Greg, what are we going to do?'

He shrugs. 'I'm guessing the coppers will want to chat to this bunch so we'll just have to let them stay.'

I groan and want to protest but I know he's right.

'Go take a quick shower and I'll make you a cuppa.'

'Thanks, Greg.' I definitely wasn't going to argue with that offer.

When I get to my room, there's a text from Joseph.

Connecting flight in Melbourne delayed. Joey.

Well that's some good news I guess. But he'll hear what's happened sooner or later.

First. Shower.

Chapter 31

Jocelyn

When we wake up to our last morning on the retreat, it's not at our own leisure, it's to frantic knocking at our door. Well, at least that's how Andy woke up. I hadn't gone to sleep yet. How was I supposed to sleep after what I witnessed last night? I hadn't told Andy, I don't know why. I should have called the police but then they might ask why I was out there and my answer isn't exactly making me look innocent.

When I open the door, Greg stands there looking as though he's pulled an all-nighter and could vomit on our doorstep at any moment. He looks exactly how I feel.

'Hi,' he says, before swallowing. 'Um, look you guys need to be in the dining room in ten minutes. Change of plans. Thanks.'

Then he walks away before I even have a chance to question him.

'What was that?' Andy asks from the bed.

I shrug. 'We need to be at the dining room in ten. No idea why.'

'It's check out day. We need to pack. There are no activities planned.'

I nod in agreement. Even though I have a pretty good idea about why things have changed.

When we get to the dining room, all the other guests are there. We'd all had to pass Celia's room on our way and the police cars were hard to miss so the whispers were running rampant.

Andy and I spot Tanner and Nadia at the same table we'd sat at last night. Lachy isn't there this time though. He must still be on his way over. We take our seats.

'What's going on?' I ask, hoping it sounds genuine.

'We probably shouldn't talk about it,' Tanner says matter-of-factly.

I scrunch my face up. 'Why?'

'Well, if there's been a crime, it's best we don't talk about it. The police should hear from all of us first.'

Right. He's in cop mode. Boring.

I glance at Nadia hoping she'll offer me something but she just smiles and shrugs.

The police officers insist on speaking to Andy and I separately. In fact, everyone is being spoken to individually and no one is allowed to leave the retreat until they've been cleared by the police. The only information we are given is that Celia was assaulted in her room overnight and has been taken to hospital. I try to appear as shocked as everyone else at the news.

What was once Celia's makeshift therapy room, is now a police interview room. Although the officers have informed us that it's *not* an interview. Not at this stage anyway. It's just an informal chat to see if we know anything, saw anything or heard anything. We all wait in the dining room, eating breakfast until we're called in by the detective.

Most people look relaxed while they eat their perfectly round pancakes topped with fruit, honeycomb crumble and a passionfruit coulis. It seems the chef hasn't been bothered by the news and is still putting up his best work.

I, on the other hand, can't bring myself to eat. Someone in this room pushed Celia and I saw it. And to make matters worse, I think someone saw me out there.

I glance around the room, trying to appear calm. It's all the same people we've eaten with every mealtime, minus Celia, her manager, Megan, and Lachy. I don't know where he is. Perhaps he checked out early before he even knew what had happened.

The only person who isn't chatting away and stuffing their face with delicious food is Kitty. She's sitting on her own at a table sobbing into her phone. One of the final things she said last night was a toast to "shitty best friends". Maybe that was the alcohol speaking because she is a mess right now.

I want to approach her or comfort her, but I feel like I could break if I move. As far as everyone knows, I was in my bed next to Andy all night.

'Hey,' Andy says, placing a hand on my thigh. 'You okay? You haven't touched your food. It's your last chance to eat like royalty.'

I offer him a half smile. 'I'm fine. Just not hungry.'

'Do you mind then?' he asks, gesturing at my plate, hoping to eat my breakfast as well as his own.

'Go for it.' I'm relieved he doesn't press any further. He also hasn't mentioned anything about last night so I assume he doesn't remember waking very briefly when I came in. I hope he doesn't remember because that's my alibi.

A short, thin woman with wild curly hair enters the dining room. She's been coming in and out, calling on guests and disappearing with them. Sometimes for a few minutes, other times a bit longer.

'Jocelyn Murphy,' she calls.

My body freezes. *Shit*. It's my turn.

I take a deep breath and try to remind myself that I didn't do anything wrong. I don't want to say I saw it happen because how do I explain why I was watching her in the bushes? That just makes me look even more guilty. I just have to hope and pray that Andy says I was with him the whole time.

Andy gives me a peck on the cheek and says, 'Good luck.'

I know that it's just a saying in jest but if only he realised, I actually do need some luck.

I smile and walk over to the woman.

'Jocelyn?'

I nod.

'I'm Detective Marie Watts, follow me.'

I take a seat opposite her. This time I'm sitting in Celia's spot while her and a colleague sit where Andy and I were seated in our counselling sessions.

'Jocelyn,' the detective says, writing on a notepad in her lap. 'As I said, I'm Detective Watts but you can call me Marie and this is Senior Sergeant Kirk. We're from the Tweed-Byron Police District and we're just asking all the guests a few questions.'

I nod, hoping they don't notice the way my hands are gripped to one another so tightly to hide the fact they're trembling.

'Last night Ms Marsden was attacked between midnight and seven am. Where were you between those hours?'

'In my room, in bed.'

'Can anyone vouch for that?' she asks, jotting down my response.

'My husband, Andy Murphy.'

She nods as she scribbles away.

Then she looks up at me and her eyes have taken on a more serious look. 'Now, I understand you and Ms Marsden did not get along this weekend. Is that right?'

How the hell does she know that? Must be some big mouths amongst the other guests. Although, all the crazy stuff from this weekend is doing the rounds on socials so it probably wouldn't be hard to research.

'Um, yes. Ah, we had a misunderstanding, I suppose you'd call it.'

'Can you elaborate?'

'There was a note left in my room, among other things, with information only Celia knew about. It was—' I sigh, 'quite disturbing.'

'And were you angry?'

'Well, yes,' I snap, before quickly steadying myself. *Shit.* 'Yes,' I say more calmly this time. 'I was very emotional about my fertility issues and it was a huge invasion of privacy. We also felt like we were being watched and judged.'

'Some guests noticed you drinking a lot last night with your husband and some other guests, and that you were talking about Celia.'

Are we in school? Bloody dobbers.

'We were certainly blowing off some steam. But the conversation was harmless.'

The detective nods, writing more notes. The other officer hasn't said a word. In fact, he's barely moved. He just sits, staring at me with an intensity I hadn't realised until now. I shift in my seat, feeling very uncomfortable.

'After having drinks last night, where did you go?' Detective Watts asked.

'Back to our room. Andy and I were in bed before midnight.'

'Midnight? You're sure?'

Yes, I'm sure because I got up just after midnight to confront Celia.

'Yes, certain. I remember seeing the time because I knew we'd have an early morning of packing ahead and was relieved it wasn't too late.' I'm shocked by how easily the lie comes.

Detective Watts smiles. 'Thank you, Ms Murphy. My colleague and I would appreciate if you delay your departure until we've spoken to a few more people.'

'But, I've seen other people leave,' I say, my voice high-pitched. 'Am I in trouble?'

'No, not at this stage.'

My heart races. *Not at this stage.* What the hell does that mean? I didn't do anything wrong. Maybe I should have just told the truth. But now that would look really bad.

I leave the room and head back to Andy in the dining room. He's laughing with Nadia and Tanner, completely oblivious to the responsibility in his hands.

Chapter 32

Nadia

Jocelyn comes back from her chat with the police and she's as white as a ghost. It makes me nervous because I thought these were just informal conversations but something has definitely spooked her.

I can't wait to get mine over and done with so I can get out of here. Tanner's mate is going to take me home, I'm basically on the way. When I texted Mum this morning letting her know I didn't need to be picked up, she bombarded me with a thousand questions. That was before I even knew about Celia and probably before any news of it had hit the media. I'm sure my phone will run hot and my mother will have plenty to say when she finds out.

I'm glad though that I'll get some extra time with Tanner before we have to say goodbye. We've agreed to try and make it work. How it'll look, I'm not sure. Especially after last night and his odd behaviour after we had sex. The worst part about that, though, is that I can't say where he was last night. I don't want to lie for him because I technically already have a criminal record and don't want to make things worse for myself. But I know he's innocent. He's a police officer and he's gentle and genuine. He wouldn't hurt anyone.

In saying that, though, I can't shake the tiny feeling of unease when I think about how angry he was at Celia's Q&A session the other night.

No, it's silly. We'd just had the most incredible evening together. His mind wouldn't have been focusing on all the drama that had taken place on this retreat. The retreat had been a blessing in disguise for both of us.

'Nadia Lombardi.' The woman who has just returned with Joss calls my name.

Once we're seated, she gets straight into it and I'm a little taken aback.

'Where were you between midnight and seven am Miss Lombardi?'

'In bed.' My voice is barely audible and I'm suddenly nauseous from the nerves.

'You've been listed as a single on our guest-list,' she says and I feel a glimmer of hope. Maybe they won't expect Tanner and I to vouch for one another. Then I don't have to choose between lying to the police or throwing the guy I like under the bus. 'But some guests mentioned you've been spending a lot of time with another guest.' She looks down at her notepad. 'A Tanner Robinson?'

Dammit.

My cheeks flush. How embarrassing. I probably look like a blushing teenager admitting to her friend that she likes someone. *Ugh.*

Stuff it. I'll tell the truth.

'Yes, Tanner and I have been hanging out a lot.'

'Including last night?'

Nosey much? 'Yes.'

'Was he with you between the hours of midnight and seven?' she asks, her eyes laced with judgement. I wonder what she's judging me about. The fact that I came here single and started hooking up with a guy. Or has she checked my background and knows I have a drink driving charge?

'Yes, we spent the night together.' I don't meet her eyes as I say it.

'The entire time?'

My mind bounces back and forth rapidly. Truth or lie. Truth or lie. If I tell her he was there the whole time and Tanner tells the truth, then I'm a liar. If I tell her Tanner left for a bit, they'll think he's a suspect. Mum's nagging voice fills my head and I remember everything her and Dad have done to get me back on my feet.

'No. He stepped out for some fresh air. Just for a minute.'

She writes something down on a notepad. 'What time was that?'

I shrug. 'Around midnight. I'm not certain.'

The detective looks up. 'Thank you. Please don't leave the resort yet. We may have some more questions.'

No doubt she will.

When I re-enter the dining room, I avoid Tanner's gaze. I've just let him down. Thrown him to the wolves. Our little love story will be over before it even properly begins.

Chapter 33

Jocelyn

'Can I get you something to drink?' Molly says, as she walks by Andy and me at the pool.

We're officially staying another night in this crazy place. I'm feeling no better than I was this morning. I managed a croissant at lunch and napped by the pool most of the afternoon. Andy is in good spirits though. He thinks we've won the jackpot—an extended holiday free of charge.

Glancing at my watch, I look up to Molly and smile. 'A glass of sparkling wine if that's okay?'

'Bit early isn't it?' Andy asks.

'It's three,' I say, 'and we're on holiday, remember?'

This seems to placate him because he orders himself a beer. He doesn't realise that the only reason I've ordered a drink is to try and calm down. The anxiety bubbling away inside me is almost too much to handle. The only reason I've managed to nap is because I'm so exhausted from last night. But when I'm awake, my chest is tight, my stomach is churning and I can't stop biting my nails.

Nadia and Tanner are by the pool too, along with Mr and Mrs Lambert and another older couple, and Kitty is sitting at the bar. She says she's waiting for the police to take her to the hospital, but I think she was asked to stay as well. The eight of us paying retreat guests are here, I assume, because we were targeted by whoever was leaving notes or stealing items from rooms. We have a motive. But I think Kitty makes a ninth person with a motive. She was pretty angry last night and perhaps today's performance was just crocodile tears.

Nevertheless, we've all had our stay extended while the police follow some other leads. At the moment, those leads include some uniformed officers performing searches of our rooms. If it helps find the creep who left me notes and ovulation tests, I'm all for staying.

'I'm just going to the bathroom,' I tell Andy, and he nods and keeps reading a book.

As I pass the bar, Greg and Molly are having a whispered exchange. Molly's face is ashen, as though she's just rediscovered Celia on the floor of her room. Kitty hasn't noticed them but I can't take my eyes off the pair. Greg has definitely just told her something. Something big.

I stand behind a pillar a few metres from them. I can no longer see them from here but I can just make out their whispered conversation.

'What do you mean they've found listening devices?' Molly hisses.

'That's what the cops were saying.' Greg sounds far more relaxed than his colleague, just like he's relaying a drinks order.

'But where?'

'One in Celia's room and another in that Murphy couple's room.'

I gasp and cover my mouth. *Please tell me they didn't hear me.*

They begin talking again and my heartrate continues racing as I try to deal with my shock. Someone has been listening to Andy and I. Listening to everything. Including when we had sex.

I swallow back warm saliva. Now is not the time to vomit. I focus on breathing deeply.

'They're also tracking down Lachy because he checked out early. But that guy was harmless. I told them as much. I mean he could kill you with his conversation skills but the man wouldn't hurt anyone.'

It is strange that Lachy is already gone. It was hard to see but the person who attacked Celia was much smaller I thought. Maybe he was the person I could hear in the bushes? Did he see the attacker? Did he see me?

There's a pop of a bottle followed by the sound of pouring liquid. Our drinks. That means Molly will be on the move any moment now. I creep to the bathrooms, satisfied they didn't see me at all.

I have so much to tell Andy now. Someone was listening to us. And it sounds like someone was listening to Celia too. Maybe she wasn't the one leaving the notes.

Chapter 34

Nadia

My phone rings for the third time in as many minutes. I'm going to have to answer. There's no avoiding this conversation.

'Hi, Mum,' I say, answering her call.

'Nadia, what's going on? Celia Marsden is in hospital after being attacked in her room at the retreat. They say she'll be fine but my God, what on earth has happened there?' I hold the phone inches from my ear because her words are becoming louder and more high-pitched by the second. 'Are you safe? Your father and I will drive there right now. Nadia? Are you listening?'

I press the button for speakerphone like usual. 'Mum, it's fine. I'm safe. The police are here. I'm staying an extra night while they keep investigating.'

'Why are you staying? I saw on Instagram that a woman posted that she got to leave the retreat and that she saw Celia get put into an ambulance. Why aren't you leaving too?'

I was worried she'd find out that only some of us were made to stay. Those of us who had an argument with her or had notes left or things taken were all told to stick around.

'It's all good. I promise. Remember, I told you there was a note in my room? I just have to stay in case it's connected. Lots of us are here. It's no big deal.'

It's a lie since I do feel as though I'm a suspect and there's a viral video of me yelling at Celia. Things don't look amazing on my part.

Mum starts rambling in Italian to my dad. I pick up a few words here and there. 'In arresto.'

'Mum!' My cheeks redden from the frustration. 'I'm not under arrest. I've literally taken your call, while sitting by the pool with a cocktail in my hand. Does that sound like I've been arrested?'

'Oh Nadia, darling, are you sure you should be drinking?'

I inwardly groan. *Is she serious?* Get off my back for one second.

'I have to go,' I say. 'I'll see you tomorrow.'

'Don't do anything stupid. And be careful.'

I hang up without saying anything. Tanner gets out of the pool in front of me. We've been switching between lounging in the sun and swimming all afternoon. If it weren't for the massive cloud of tension hanging in the air between us, it'd almost be romantic and relaxing. But the cloud is there and it is thick, grey and ready to burst.

Since Tanner came back from his chat with the detective, he's been quiet. Even quieter than usual. Perhaps, I'm just paranoid and reading too much into it but I think he's pissed off that I said what I did to the cops. But he's a police officer. Surely he understands why I told the truth, and if he's innocent, why is he worried?

'Was the water nice?' I ask, even though I've been in the pool several times myself already.

'Mmm.'

'Did you want another beer?'

'I'll go.'

These short interactions have been the story of our afternoon. I can't take it anymore.

'Wait, Tanner. Is everything okay?'

He doesn't look at me.

'Is it because I told the police you went for fresh air during the night? I'm sorry, I didn't mean to throw you under the bus.' I'm rambling. 'But you know, I have a history and I don't want to get into any trouble. Please understand—.'

'Stop,' he cuts me off. 'I'm not mad at you for telling the truth. I would expect you to, encourage you to.'

'Then why has it been so weird since I spoke to the police, since last night even?'

He sits on the lounge next to me, still dripping wet from the pool. Then he takes my hand in his. 'Nadia, do you think I did it?'

He looks me right in the eye and I can see the emotion there. But I'm still not sure what I've done to upset him. I shake my head but no words come.

'But you don't know where I was.'

I think back to last night. I'd been so upset when he left the room. I felt like a failure, rejected. 'I didn't want to know.'

'Because you think I did it,' he says.

I shake my head. 'No. Not that. I thought you must be off, I don't know, calling a mate to tell them how rubbish I was or calling your ex to say how no one compares to her.'

Tanner laughs and I glare at him. This is not funny.

'Well, this is a misunderstanding,' he says and I raise my eyebrows waiting for him to elaborate. 'I thought you weren't asking me because you were worried I was guilty and that upset me that you didn't trust me. But that's not it at all.' He places a hand on my cheek and kisses my lips softly. 'Nadia, last night was perfect. I wouldn't change a thing.'

'Really?' I ask. 'Then why leave?'

'Because as perfect as it was, it was also overwhelming.' He takes a deep breath and his cheeks flush a deep red. 'I haven't had sex since my wife left me. I have barely felt anything since she left. Now you're here

and my mind is racing and I'm feeling everything so hard. It's just—'
He lets out a long breath. 'A lot.'

I smile and a tear rolls down my cheek. I should have just asked him.

'I get it,' I say. Then he kisses me again.

The Lambert couple, who are two bottles of chardonnay deep, whistle. Usually, I'd be mortified but I'm done with hiding. This man can kiss me where he wants, for as long as he wants.

Or at least until the police return for us.

We're halfway through dinner, when Detective Watts enters the dining room. She's certainly not as fresh-eyed as she looked this morning and her bouncy curls from earlier are now pulled back in a frizzy ponytail. It's been a big day.

'Thank you all for waiting around,' she announces to the room. 'We're still investigating and we're grateful to Molly for extending your stay.' I glance around at everyone. It's the same group minus Kitty who has been taken to the hospital to be with Celia.

Molly smiles from the corner of the room but it's clear she isn't thrilled about it. Offering her rooms and services for a night for free was probably not her idea. I imagine the police don't want to send a group of drunken potential suspects out into the greedy hands of the media who have been set up out the front since this afternoon.

Joss raises her hand like a child in a classroom and the detective nods at her.

'Um, so who did it then?' Jocelyn slurs, the afternoon of alcohol catching up with her.

'We haven't arrested anyone at this stage.'

'But?' Joss continues to pry.

'Nothing else to add.' The detective turns to leave and then stops. She faces us again. 'Wait, there is one thing.' She pulls out a plastic evidence bag from her pocket. 'Has anyone seen this before?'

The gold pen shines in the light of the dining room. I recognise it straight away. Not just because I found it funny when Lachy gave it to her on the first night because that is exactly something my mum would do, but because Celia then used it during our session.

'That's the pen she used during our therapy sessions,' Andy says, before I get a chance to.

'Why?' Tanner asks, from his seat next to me.

'I'm not able to share that information. But thank you, that's very helpful.'

Retreat for Couples and Divorcees Turns Violent: Celia Marsden Assaulted

By Joseph Anderson

November 16th, 2022

In a shocking turn of events, what was meant to be a peaceful retreat for couples and divorcees took a grim twist as special guest Celia Marsden was assaulted in her suite. The serene setting of the retreat, located in the picturesque Tweed-Byron area, has now become a crime scene, with local authorities racing to unravel the mystery behind the attack.

Trouble had been brewing in the days leading up to the assault, with guests sharing accounts of escalating conflicts and tension on social media. Arguments involving Celia Marsden and other attendees had become apparent.

The assault itself has left the retreat's participants in a state of shock and fear. Police have been questioning attendees extensively, leading to an extension of their stay, as they work to identify the assailant, who may still be among them.

Social media platforms are awash with posts and comments from retreat-goers and observers, further complicating the situation with accusations and speculations.

The resort, known for its breathtaking ocean views, now stands as a stark reminder of the hidden tensions that can boil over into violence even in the most tranquil settings.

As the investigation continues, the community eagerly awaits answers regarding what truly transpired.

Chapter 35

Detective Marie Watts

This used to be such a beautiful and quiet region. I've been a police officer in the Tweed-Byron district for thirty years but the last ten years have been a whole new ballgame. The influx of tourists, people relocating here, and don't get me started on the celebrities and influencers— who've decided this peaceful neck of the woods is the perfect place to take their selfies.

The increase in population means an increase in crime. And that means more stress on what is a pretty small police department. Like most things, funding from the government never quite keeps up with the speed of society. We're understaffed, under-resourced and just plain fed up.

'Okay, I've got an address linked to the credit card,' Senior Sergeant Bob Kirk says, from near his computer.

We're back at the station now, after a long day at the Sand & Salt Resort. Bob's another one of the *oldies,* as they call us here at the station. He transferred from Sydney twenty years ago for a quieter lifestyle. Didn't that backfire?

'Hit me, Bob.'

As soon as we'd found listening devices at the resort, including inside some rooms, we'd spoken to Molly. She was quick to identify the pen as being one that was gifted to Celia. The pen was a recording device. Everywhere Celia took it, someone was listening. It explained the mystery of how someone knew about the Lambert's golf habit and the Murphy's fertility struggles. It was sick. And Lachy was behind it all.

We'd managed to find the credit card he'd used in Molly's computer records and now Bob had an address. *Lachy, we're coming for you.*

'The address is Squire Drive in Suffolk Park. The house is rented by a Jeremy Lachlan Manningham.'

'So Jeremy is going by his middle name these days,' I ponder. 'Suffolk Park isn't far. Let's go.'

'Wait,' Bob says. 'There's more.'

I sigh. 'There always is. What's young Jeremy been up to?'

'There is an apprehended domestic violence order against him. His ex-wife had one put in place for...' Bob reads the screen, scrolling the mouse. 'Stalking.' He shrugs. 'Sounds like we've found ourselves a doozy. Let's go then.'

Jeremy Manningham's house is a small place about a kilometre inland from the beach. It's a rundown weatherboard in desperate need of a fresh coat of paint. The lawn is overgrown and his car sits under a rusty old carport.

'You'd think someone who can afford a retreat at a resort would live somewhere nicer,' Bob remarks, as we pull up.

'Not everyone cares about *stuff*. Personally, give me memories over tangible items,' I say and Bob shrugs. 'Now remember,' I add, 'we're just here to take him in for questioning. We don't have a warrant for a search yet.'

As we approach the front door, Bob stops. 'Do you smell that?'

It's smoke. I nod and look around for the source of it. It's late, too late for a barbecue I would've thought, and definitely too warm for a fireplace. Then I see the smoke rising from behind the house.

'Round back,' I say quietly.

Thankfully, the house is so rundown that there is no fence separating the front and backyards. We just have to march through the tall grass. It really is a hazard to be lighting a fire with this much dry grass around and next to a weatherboard.

As I round the back corner of the house, the source of the smoke greets me. A makeshift fire pit has been set up in the middle of the backyard using an old steel drum. But Jeremy is nowhere to be seen.

The backdoor of the house slams shut and out he comes carrying a cardboard box.

'Freeze!' I shout and move into his line of sight. 'This is the police.' I haven't got my weapon drawn but I strongly suspect that he is about to burn something he doesn't want people to know about. Especially us.

He sees us and scrambles toward the fire.

Bob bounds past me and tackles him to the grass before he reaches it. The box goes flying, its contents spilling. We may not have a warrant but now we suspect someone of trying to destroy evidence, that changes everything. Bob cuffs him while I quickly snap on some evidence gloves and collect items from the grass around us.

I pick up a few loose pieces of paper before they can fly away. Then my eyes are drawn to the largest item to fall out of the box. A familiar face stares up at me from the back cover of a paperback. I turn it over. It's a copy of *Loveless Marriage* by Celia Marsden.

Opening the book, I discover it's covered in annotations scribbled across most of the pages. Not just any annotations though, the words are angry and vile. *Lying bitch. Brainwashed. Home wrecker.* Someone certainly took their anger out on this book.

I flick through the loose pages. There are printouts of local resorts, including Sand & Salt. There are emails to several resorts and to Celia's manager suggesting a retreat for couples. There are photos of Celia and her family, and printouts of some of her social media posts. And there's a photo of a younger looking Jeremy standing hand in hand with a woman in a wedding dress.

Bob is pulling Jeremy to his feet. His eyes grow wide when he sees me collecting the evidence.

'It's not what it looks like,' he says.

'And what does it look like?' Bob asks, having just reminded Jeremy of his rights and Jeremy clearly ignoring his right to remain silent.

'You have to believe me,' he continues to plead.

'Let's talk about this at the station,' I say.

Chapter 36

Detective Marie Watts

Jeremy Lachlan Manningham looks terrified sitting in the interview room at the station. We are yet to formally speak with him because we're still examining all the evidence we found. Based on the emails Jeremy printed, it seems he was very keen to get Celia up to the Northern Rivers area. He had posted reviews on several local resorts highlighting their suitability for a retreat and even specifically mentioned Celia Marsden in some of them. Plus, he'd used a range of fake usernames to contact Celia as a nasty troll, a fan of her work and as someone desperate for an event aimed at new divorcees.

'This is the problem with the internet,' I say to no one, leafing through all of the papers one last time before we question him. 'You can pretend to be anyone.'

Bob enters the room.

'So are we ready to go?' I ask.

'One last thing. I've just got off the phone with Mrs Manningham, or rather the ex-Mrs Manningham. Her name is Louisa, lovely lady.'

'And?' Bob's great but he can make a thirty second update into a five minute lecture if I don't keep him on track.

'They divorced some years back and she had an apprehended domestic violence order taken out when he continued to show up unwelcome and unannounced at her home and workplace. He would beg her to take him back and when she asked him to leave, he would become threatening.'

'Of course he did. Anything related to Ms Marsden?'

'Well, this is where it gets interesting,' Bob says, raising an eyebrow. 'Louisa had been miserable for a while and read Celia's book in the hope of repairing her marriage but instead she realised—'

'Bob, I don't have time for Louisa's midlife crisis story. What's the link?'

'Basically she left Jeremy after being inspired by the book. She told him he should read it and that it may help him understand but it would seem Louisa has innocently thrown poor Ms Marsden under the bus and now he blames Celia for the divorce.'

I run a hand through my hair. 'Well, there's his motive. And this evidence is pretty telling. Let's have a chat with him.'

Jeremy's a picture of panic when we enter. His eyes are wide and he's rocking on the spot, unable to stay still. Before we can take a seat opposite him, he speaks.

'I didn't do this. You have to believe me.'

Bob and I sit on the other side of the table. I place a folder with all the evidence we've collected in front of me and rest my hands on top.

'Mr Manningham, where were you between midnight last night and seven this morning?'

He says nothing. Just stares at his hands, his thumbs frantically squeezing his knuckles so they turn white.

'Is it true your wife left you after reading *Loveless Marriage*?' Bob asks. He's agreed to play bad cop today.

Jeremy's head snaps up and his cheeks redden. 'Who said that?'

'I had a nice chat with your ex-wife, Louisa, before. Lovely woman, seems very smart,' he taunts.

Jeremy slams his palms on the table. 'Don't say another word about Louisa.'

'Oooo,' Bob says, raising two hands up in front of him. 'I can see why she had to have an order placed against you.'

Jeremy's hands grip at the table. I turn to Bob and give him a slight nod to indicate 'that's enough'.

'Jeremy, I'm going to ask you again,' I say, calmly. 'Where were you last night between midnight and seven?'

Jeremy runs his hands through his hair before pulling at it in frustration. Then he exhales loudly. 'I know it looks bad. I admit that I tried to get Celia up here for a retreat. I emailed about hosting a conference or event and then all the influencers were up here spruiking resorts and wellness retreats so I thought it might tempt her.'

'Why did you want to get her here?'

'I wanted to ask her how she felt about destroying so many relationships. Whenever I asked on social media, she'd delete my comment or if I emailed her, she ignored it. She ruined my life and I wanted answers. I needed to see her in person.'

'Did you want revenge?'

Jeremy's face twists. 'No. I didn't touch her.'

'Why were you listening in on Celia's sessions?'

'I just wanted to scare her and the guests a bit. Cause some tension so that her image wasn't so picture bloody perfect.'

'Look, we have a lot of evidence—evidence you attempted to destroy—suggesting you hate Celia. Another guest saw you leave your room just before midnight and you left the resort before the retreat ended. It doesn't look good,' I say.

He squeezes his eyes closed. 'I don't know what to tell you. It wasn't me.'

'Mr Manningham,' Bob says. 'We have enough to charge you with stalking, and you've admitted to the break and enters at the retreat. I suggest you cooperate because this isn't looking good for you.'

Jeremy puts his elbows on the table and his head in his hands.

Bob and I leave the interview room and slump into seats in my office.

'What are you thinking, boss?' he asks.

'It seems so obvious right?'

He nods.

'My gut says it's too obvious,' I add.

'Sometimes it's just that cut and dry.'

I shrug. 'I'm going to get some rest and then make some more calls.'

'What am I doing with him?' he asks, pointing in the direction of the interview room.

I glance at my watch. 'We can't keep him much longer without charging him. Start with the charges for stalking Ms Marsden and for the breaks ins, and then release him. I don't think he's a threat now she's in the hospital.'

It's a short drive back to my own place and my mind races through the different people I spoke to today. The retreat had clearly not gone well and there are lots of reasons why the guests would be annoyed at Celia. But what about Molly? Her resort was getting lots of publicity at the moment and it was not positive. Plus, if someone with Celia's reach was to speak negatively about her time at Sand & Salt, that would be bad news for Molly.

Chapter 37

Molly

I climb into bed late with a bottle of red wine. Just when I thought things couldn't get worse here, they did.

Not only did Sand & Salt host a disaster of a retreat, we're receiving negative publicity, there's been an assault on the premises and now I'm putting up guests free of charge.

I don't even bother with a glass, I just take swigs straight from the bottle. The crimson liquid covers the back of my hand as I wipe it from my lips. *What a mess.*

Joseph had arrived this afternoon, much to my horror. However, he's been very pleasant so far. I imagine it's for the sake of the guests and the police. I suspect my life as I know it is a ticking time bomb and Joey holds the detonator.

My head is pounding when my alarm goes off in the morning. I fumble with my phone before my foggy brain realises it's not my phone alerting me. It's the alarm I have on the motion sensor outside the reception building. Because I live above reception, I installed it so I'd know if anyone was coming. I open the app on my phone that shows live footage of the area just outside reception and there stands the detective from yesterday.

It's six-thirty, is she serious? I can only hope she's here to tell me this nightmare is over and I can send everyone home.

I sway on my feet as I stand up. Then I pop a few paracetamol tablets before wrapping a robe around myself and heading downstairs.

Detective Marie Watts looks as exhausted as I feel.

'Good morning,' she says. 'Sorry to bother you so early.'

'That's okay,' I lie. 'How can I help? Do you need to speak to one of the guests?'

'Actually, no. I was hoping to have a word with you.'

I narrow my eyes. *Really? Have I not done enough to help?* 'Sure. Can I get dressed and meet you in the dining room? I need to start preparing for the guests to wake up.'

'Of course.' She smiles.

I race upstairs and get ready. I can't help but feel a little uneasy at the detective's words. *Actually, I was hoping to have a word with you.* Does she think I know something?

By the time I'm dressed and walking over to the dining room, I've managed to convince myself that I'm the number one suspect and that I'll be adding "criminal" next to "unemployed" on my bio.

'Thanks for this,' Detective Watts says. 'I know it's early but I have a few questions.'

I nod and we sit down at one of the tables. This is casual, I think to myself. She's surely not going to interrogate me and arrest me after a casual chat like this.

'How did you feel about Celia coming here for the *Loveless Marriage* retreat?' she asks.

Terrified. Nervous. 'Excited,' I lie again. What is wrong with me? 'Seemed like a great way to show off our facilities here.'

She nods, taking notes in a notebook she brought with her. 'So, it must have been stressful when guests and Celia herself were unhappy with how the retreat was going?'

'Yeah, I suppose so. But those things had nothing to do with the resort.'

'You don't think the security of the rooms here is the responsibility of the resort?'

My face flushes. 'Of course it is. I just mean—'

'You must've been upset that Celia's retreat exposed the lack of security here,' she says, cutting me off.

I say nothing. A sick feeling weighs heavy in my stomach. She's created my motive.

'Where were you during the time of the attack?' Detective Watts asks.

'After I finished cleaning in here', I gesture at the room around us. 'I went straight to bed.'

'Can anyone vouch for that?'

I think for a moment. Then it hits me. The exact same way I knew the detective had arrived this morning.

'Yes, I have surveillance set up around the reception building, they're motion sensored. You'll see when I enter and exit on the recording.'

She raises her eyebrows and nods.

'I'd like to have a look at that footage, if possible.'

'Of course.'

Detective Watts stands up.

Before she can leave, I speak up. 'Can I check out the guests this morning?'

'Let's make it a late check out,' she says. 'I'm not quite finished with them yet.'

I force a smile as she walks away.

An extra night and a late check out, plus you have the nerve to accuse me of assaulting a guest. Is it too early for another drink?

Chapter 38
Detective Marie Watts

My phone buzzes as I walk into the station. It's an email from Molly with some video files attached. I'll have forensics look over them but I suspect she's telling the truth. I also suspect she'd love to attack me from behind but I'm not here to make everyone's life easy. I'm here to solve a crime.

Jeremy's court appearance isn't for a few weeks but Bob is convinced he'll be pleading not guilty to stalking. And if we manage to hit him with the assault charge, he'll deny that too. On paper, it's an open and close case. There's motive, opportunity and plenty of incriminating evidence. But my gut isn't so sure.

There's something about his behaviour. It's as though he's frustrated because he didn't get to attack her. Like he had orchestrated everything and was ready to go but someone got there first.

I make myself a coffee and sit at my desk. Flicking through my notebook, I wait for something to jump out at me. Jocelyn and Andy have one another as their alibi. Tanner left briefly but I spoke to some of his colleagues in Brisbane. They reckon he wouldn't hurt a fly. Plus, who has sex and then gets the sudden urge to attack someone? I'm not buying it. Nadia was asleep in bed, which is confirmed except for when Tanner left. She has a record but it's for drink driving. Nothing violent. Plus she was happy to throw her lover under the bus to tell the truth. I don't think she has it in her. Every other client of Celia's has an alibi.

Client. Shit. I'd missed it. Kitty Anh is Celia's friend from Melbourne. She wasn't there as a paying guest in need of Celia's services. But one of the guests had said they'd heard her bad mouthing her so-called friend at the final dinner. We didn't speak to her yesterday, she'd been so distraught by the attack on her friend that she slipped under our radar.

I dial Bob's number.

'Hey, boss,' he says.

'You on your way in?' I ask.

'Around the corner. What's up?'

'Whatever happened with Kitty Anh yesterday? She was the distraught friend.'

'Yep, I know the one. Constable Reid dropped her at the hospital on his way back to the station. That's all I know.'

'I think we need to have a chat with her.'

'I'll go and see her.'

He hangs up just as the station receptionist pops her head into my office.

'Detective, a Jeremy Manningham is at the desk asking to speak with you.'

I jump out of my seat and follow her out to the waiting area. Jeremy stands behind the counter wearing the same clothing he had on last night. His eyes are bloodshot and a five o'clock shadow covers his face.

'Jeremy, your court date isn't for several weeks. What brings you here?'

'Can we speak in private?'

I lead him into the same interview room we used last night.

'Are you here to confess?' I ask.

'No. Well, not to the attack. I was near Celia's room when she was pushed.'

I sit up a little straighter.

'I,' he sighs. 'I was watching her.'

I raise my eyebrows. 'Watching her from where?'

He looks down at his hands. 'From the bushes. I was trying to work up the courage to properly confront her.'

'And you did that by spying on her?'

'Well no. I never got the courage. She was so drunk and I didn't think I'd get the answers I was after. But I couldn't leave.'

'Why not?' I ask.

'Because I'm not the only person who was out there. I didn't want to be seen.'

'You mean her attacker? Did you see them?'

'No,' he says. 'I saw Jocelyn. I don't know why she was out there but we were both outside when Celia was attacked. I think Joss saw me. Or heard me.'

'Wait a minute. You mean two of you witnessed the attack?'

Jeremy nods.

'And neither of you shouted for help or called the police? She could've died in there.'

He bites his lip. 'I know. I can't speak for Jocelyn, but for me, I was scared. What if the attacker saw me and I was next? And how would I explain what I was doing?'

Chapter 39

Jocelyn

I assumed we were all off the hook when the detective showed us the pen last night. It wasn't difficult to put two and two together. Lachy was using that pen to listen to Celia's conversations and then terrorising the rest of us. Then he disappeared after she was attacked. He was a downright creep.

However, when we get up this morning, Detective Watts has been and gone and Molly informs us over breakfast that we won't be able to leave until at least the afternoon and that the detective would be returning again soon.

'I've got clients relying on me,' I say, thinking about the salon back at home. I'd managed to cover my appointments for today but I assumed I'd be flying home this afternoon.

'It's out of my control,' Molly responds. 'It's not exactly my preference to be putting you all up free of charge.'

My shoulders sag. I feel bad. It isn't right that Molly is having to wear the cost of this. I mean technically the cops can't force any of us to stay and they can't force Molly to host us but people are often far too scared to not do what they're told these days. Not when a statement or action could somehow end up on record, on someone's camera reel, on someone's social media. It's safest to just do as we're told.

I'm finishing off the last few bites of an incredible breakfast burrito that the chef has served us, when Detective Watts enters the dining room. My appetite had returned last night when I thought the case was solved. I dab at the runny yolk and melted cheese that spills onto my chin. Burritos are simply not a first date food—so messy. Luckily, I'm not trying to date the detective and Andy has seen me in far worse states.

She makes a bee line for our table.

'Ms Murphy,' she says, and I feel the breakfast burrito drop to the pit of my stomach. 'Can we have a word in private?'

'Is there a problem?' Andy asks.

Yes, I think to myself. *I witnessed the attack.* 'No,' I say to Andy, before the detective can speak. I squeeze his hand as I get up from my seat. 'I'm sure it's fine.'

I follow her into the same private room that I feel I've spent far more time in than I'd truly like.

'Take a seat, Ms Murphy.'

I sit opposite her. She's on her own this time but she has her notepad at the ready to take down everything.

'Last night, we arrested Jeremy Manningham. You know him as Lachy.'

I nod, trying to disguise the fact I want to ask a hundred more questions.

'He used listening devices to record Celia's sessions and there was a device found in your room.'

I clasp a hand over my mouth, pretending I hadn't already over-heard some of that information. I swallow back the burning sensation threatening to make my burrito reappear. Hearing it actually confirmed is horrifying. I feel violated. I rub at the skin on my arms, scrubbing frantically, like I'm trying to wash off the disgust and humiliation.

'Ms Murphy, I understand this is a shock. It's okay, he can't hurt you.'

I take a deep breath and slowly meet her eyes. 'Why couldn't you tell Andy and I this together? Why just me?'

'There's something else I wanted to ask.' She purses her lips together. It's as though she's mentally preparing to ask me the next question, which just makes the flips my stomach is already doing even more violent. 'Lachy claims to have not attacked Ms Marsden but that he witnessed the attack.'

My eyes widen and I quickly look down, hoping she doesn't notice. But she's a detective, of course she notices. She's trained to see these reactions.

'He also claims that you witnessed the attack. Is that true?'

I press at my temples and squeeze my eyes shut. I can't believe this is happening. Andy and I signed up for a fun and relaxing retreat where we could work on our marriage. Instead I've been personally violated and stalked, witnessed an assault, and ended up lying to the police. This is not the weekend we had planned.

When I open my eyes, a single tear rolls down my cheek and I wipe it away with a shaky hand. 'Yes, it's true,' I say, my voice barely audible.

'Why didn't you call the police? Or tell us this yesterday?'

I shrug, ashamed of myself. 'I panicked. There was someone else out there with me. I guess Lachy, according to what he said to you, but I didn't see him, just heard him. What if he was in on it? Or if the attacker saw me? I was scared. I panicked and ran back to my room.'

'Did you see the attacker?'

'No, it was too dark.'

'Did you tell Andy what happened?'

I shake my head quickly. 'No, no. Please don't question him again. He has no idea.'

'What were you doing outside Celia's room that evening?'

My heart rate rises. This whole conversation is going to kill me, my body is in a state of fear. I'm sure the detective can hear the racing of my heartbeat.

'Well,' I croak. 'I was upset. I needed to know if it was her who left the stuff in our room.'

'So you hid in the bushes?'

I look down. 'I started at the front door and then heard her around the back. When I got there, she was a mess. Super drunk. So I hid and filmed her on my phone. I thought I could then get some answers out of her, or maybe even a refund or something, if I threatened to share the videos.'

'Do you still have the videos?'

'Yeah. But you can't see anything. I'd stopped recording.'

'Nevertheless, I'd like a copy for evidence. We might be able to pick something up you didn't notice.'

'Of course.' I fidget with my wedding band. 'Am I going to be charged?'

'You've done a lot I don't agree with, Ms Murphy,' Detective Watts begins. 'I can't say for certain but because you're also a victim here and you've helped us with our investigation, be it somewhat reluctantly, hopefully I can help you out.'

I half smile. 'Thank you, detective.'

Chapter 40

Detective Marie Watts

I get back to the station at lunchtime and am relieved that Bob has bought us sandwiches. I don't care if they're pre-made from the service station, I'm ravenous. I'd been to Sand & Salt twice this morning and hadn't eaten. Molly didn't offer me any breakfast, whether that was an innocent mistake or her way of making it known she isn't happy about the current situation, I'm not sure.

'Egg and lettuce or ham and cheese?' Bob asks, holding up two plastic boxes.

'I would eat the plastic box at this stage. You choose, I'll have any.'

He hands me the ham and cheese sandwich before opening his own. Between mouthfuls I fill him in on my morning.

'That place really needs better surveillance,' Bob says. 'We've now got two people out of their rooms at the time of the attack but who claim not to be the attacker.'

'Correct. So three people were outside Celia's room at one point.'

'I'm not asking them to film their guests. Heck no. But a little camera outside the entrances and we could be eating burgers right now instead of this.' He holds up a very sloppy looking egg and lettuce sandwich. 'And when I spoke to Lachy earlier, he said that Greg was very forthcoming about the security. Straight out overshared with Lachy that there were no cameras.'

I shake my head. 'Hopeless. What happened with Kitty?'

'No one can vouch for the fact that she was in her room but her husband said he spoke to her about 11:30 to say goodnight.'

'We really need to speak to Celia.' I say, taking a sip of water. 'There are too many people with a motive and no alibi.'

'I still have my money on Lachy. He probably saw Ms Murphy from inside the room.'

I sigh. 'I don't know. He's angry and he wanted to destroy her reputation, yes. He violated people's privacy and is probably going to prison for something. But I believe him when he says he wouldn't hurt her.'

'Your gut is usually rock solid, boss. But I'm not with you this time.'

The station receptionist pops her head in.

'Marie, we just got a call from the hospital. Ms Marsden is awake and ready to talk.'

'Thanks,' I say and shove the last bit of sandwich into my mouth. 'Let's go.'

A young doctor who looks as though he just stepped off his surfboard and into his hospital scrubs greets us outside Celia's hospital room.

His long blonde hair is tied in what I've recently had described to me as a man-bun, and his scrubs have little pictures of different coloured combi vans on them. It's as if Byron Bay vomited on a doctor.

'Hi, I'm Doctor Hunter. I was here yesterday when Celia came in. She was in and out of consciousness during the drive over. When she properly woke here in hospital, she was distressed and we gave her sedatives because her heart rate and blood pressure weren't handling the stress. She needed twenty-three stitches at the back and side of her head.'

I nod, taking note of it all on my notepad. I know Doctor Hunter will share the medical reports but writing the notes has always helped me process the information better. I'm too old to change my methods now.

'Her publicist, Megan, hasn't left her side and her friend, Kitty, arrived later yesterday. I understand her husband is on his way from Melbourne. When she woke this morning from the sedation, she asked for the police. She asked for you before her husband, which the nurses and I found to be quite—'

I hold up a hand to cut him off. I'm not here for Dr Surfer-boy's opinion on his patient.

'Thanks, doctor. Can we go in?'

'Yes. Just not too long okay? She's suffered a serious concussion. She'll be tired.'

I've entered many hospital rooms as part of my job, but I've never seen anything quite like what I find in Celia's room.

Lying in her bed, slightly propped up by some pillows, is Celia. Not just any pillows though, they have silk pillowcases and I wonder who has managed to deliver those in the last twenty-four hours. Molly had mentioned that Celia is demanding but she was asleep. This must be the work of the two women with her.

Sitting in an armchair next to Celia is the woman I recognise as being frantic when the ambulance arrived yesterday. Celia's friend, Kitty. She has one of Celia's hands resting on the overbed table and is painting her nails. Yep, painting her nails. Who is this Celia woman? Next someone will be in here hand-feeding her grapes.

But it's not Kitty that has me most taken aback. On the other side of Celia, there's a small bench set up with not one, not two but three laptops and Megan is typing away at one of them, seemingly rushed. There's a tripod set up with a smartphone and a large ring light behind it. It looks like a mini recording studio.

Bob and I are silent for a moment taking it all in before Celia clears her throat.

I look back to her. For someone who is concussed, she looks immaculate. If she's only recently woken up, then she prioritised hair and make-up over calling us and apparently her family. Her hair has been parted so that it hangs heavy over one side. My guess is that's the side with the stitches.

'Ms Marsden, it's so good to see you awake. How are you feeling?' I ask.

'I've certainly felt better but at least I'm alive.' She shoots a look at Megan who ignores her.

'Do you remember anything about the attack?'

Megan looks over from the laptop but doesn't say anything.

'A little bit,' she sighs dramatically, and then wipes at a non-existent tear. 'I'd been bullied over the weekend. While I tried to selflessly help others, I had my reputation tarnished.'

I bite my teeth together to stop from laughing. This woman is a piece of work.

'Kitty, file that one down a bit more,' she barks at her friend, pointing at a fingernail. She looks back at us. 'I was devastated and had a few drinks in my room. I'd just been enjoying the view out the back and gone inside when I was pushed from behind.'

'Did you see your attacker?'

'No, as I said, the coward struck from behind.'

'Did they say anything to you?'

'Yes, they said something as they pushed me. I can't recall what but I recognised the voice.'

My eyes plead with her to continue.

'It was Lachy.'

Megan turns back to her computer as Kitty's eyes widen.

'Really?' Kitty asks.

'Unmistakable,' Celia says. 'Never forget his voice. He's so creepy.'

I put up a hand to stop Celia. This wasn't a gossip session at the nail salon. I shouldn't have even allowed this conversation to happen with the other women here.

'We'll need to get a formal statement from you, Ms Marsden,' I said.

'My husband can bring me to the station tomorrow,' she says. 'But if you don't mind now, I've got some work to do.' She gestures at the tripod and Megan and we take it as our cue to leave.

When we climb into the car, Bob starts on me. 'I told you it was him. That gut of yours is not so rock solid after all.'

I nod, reluctantly conceding defeat.

'What on earth was all that stuff in there?' he asks.

'I'm not certain but it looked like recording equipment.'

Bob lets out a huff. 'Is there any privacy these days? What, now we even have to watch someone recover in their hospital bed?'

'Who knows? Anyway, let's get back to the station and get Lachy brought in. Time to add assault to his rap sheet.'

When we get to the station, a group of officers are crowded around one of the computer screens.

'Check this out, Wattsy,' one of the young constables calls out to me.

I stand behind them. 'What is it?'

'Celia Marsden has gone live on Instagram,' the same constable says.

My eyebrows knit together and then they clarify for me.

'It means she's filming live on her Instagram and her followers can watch in real-time and comment as she speaks.'

'Right,' I say, hoping that she isn't about to jeopardise the investigation. 'So what has she said?'

'Her retreat was a set up to destroy her reputation. She was bullied, stalked and attacked by people who didn't agree with her work.'

'Wow,' I say, because I have no other word to describe the situation. She has taken this attack and turned it into an opportunity. Why am I not surprised?

Celia continues speaking to her live audience. 'I'm here to represent other artists like myself, whether they're authors, musicians, comedians, whoever you are, we deserve to be protected from trolls and stalkers. I've created a GoFundMe page, the link is in my bio and I'm raising money for awareness and support for victims of online bullying. Hopefully, no one else's attacks go from the keyboard to real life.' Celia takes a deep breath, closes her eyes and purses her lips. 'Like mine did. Thank you for tuning in, guys.' Then she blows kisses to the camera before the feed is shut off.

'She can't raise money from this, can she?' Bob asks.

The officer seated at the computer speaks up as she clicks away at the computer screen. 'She already has. The GoFundMe page is going crazy. Five grand raised already with messages calling her a hero and thanking her for her bravery.'

Bob shakes his head. 'We're living in a bloody mad world. Making money off being attacked like this. Just incredible.' His voice trails off as he heads to his office.

I go into my office too. I have to prepare to formally charge Lachy with assault.

Online Bullying Survivor, Celia Marsden, Launches GoFundMe Campaign for Awareness and Support

By Anthony Wild

November 17th, 2022

In a shocking incident at Sand & Salt Resort, Celia Marsden became the victim of a brutal assault at the weekend. As she recovers in the hospital, Celia has chosen to turn her ordeal into a platform for change.

A Survivor's Strength

Celia Marsden, a survivor of both online bullying and physical assault, is refusing to be defined by her trauma. Instead, she's using her experience to spotlight the pervasive problem of online bullying.

The GoFundMe Campaign

Celia has initiated a GoFundMe campaign titled 'War on Warriors: Ending Online Bullying and Keyboard Warriors.' This campaign has three main goals; raise awareness, support victims and research the psychology of these bullies.

How You Can Help

- Donate: Visit Celia's GoFundMe page and contribute to her cause.

- Share: Spread the word about Celia's campaign on social media and with your contacts.

- Learn: Educate yourself about the signs and consequences of online bullying.

- Support: Be an ally to those facing online harassment, offering your support.

Celia Marsden's journey from victim to advocate is a remarkable example of resilience. By supporting her campaign, we can join her in creating a safer online world for everyone.

Chapter 41

Celia

Two hours after going live on Instagram, I've raised almost twenty thousand dollars. I'm yet to work out exactly how I can spend the money for my new cause. There's a lot of psychology behind the actions of bullies so I'm sure this could be a new research project for me. Maybe, even another book.

'The Today Show and Sunrise want an interview tomorrow morning, Ceels,' Megan says, tapping away at one of the laptops.

'Lock it in,' I say, not looking at her.

'Will you speak to them from home? Isn't Tom coming soon to take you back to Melbourne?'

'No. Tell them I want to record it from here. My injuries are so bad, I must stay another night. I'll just tell that hot doctor my head still hurts too much.'

'And Tom?' Kitty asks, this time.

'He'll do whatever I tell him to.' I smile and she winces.

Kitty is so weak. I haven't forgotten that she turned on me. She came running back when she thought I was seriously hurt and hasn't left my side. I guess decades of friendship does mean something to her. I will forgive but not forget. Plus, I can't alienate my friend. Not when she knows so much about what happened on the retreat.

Kitty nods, sitting back in the arm chair. I don't think her skinny ass has left that spot since she arrived. I need a break from her.

'Kitty, honey, can you go and see if they have proper coffee here? Or maybe a cafe nearby?'

'Of course.'

'And remember, almond milk only.'

She nods and scurries away.

When the door closes, I'm alone with Megan for the first time since I woke up. I sit up a little higher in bed and then turn to her.

She's typing on the computer when she senses my eyes on her and looks at me.

'What the hell did you do?' I scowl at her.

She glances at the door and then back at me.

'Megan, what the hell came over you?'

'Celia, it's working. You've raised thousands of dollars and you've sold more copies of *Loveless Marriage* today than you have in the past six months. This is *exactly* the kind of publicity you wanted from the retreat.'

'Yes, from the retreat. Not from being assaulted. I'm lucky to be alive.'

She says nothing.

'We agreed,' I say, feeling the heat burning in my cheeks, 'that you would trash my room while I was sleeping and I would wake up terrified and the story of the retreat would be the horrible treatment of me rather than about the guests.'

Megan swallows. 'I know. But some of those guests were screwed over bad. One couple were recorded having sex. At your retreat!' She takes a deep breath. 'Trashing your room wasn't enough.'

'So you attacked me.'

'I didn't mean to hurt you so badly but you were drunk and I didn't know you'd hit your head.'

'Did you think to call an ambulance?'

'No, because I didn't realise you were hurt. It was barely a nudge.'

A nurse comes rushing in and I realise that the machine next to me is beeping loudly.

'Ms Marsden, is everything okay?' the nurse asks, checking the machine and looking at my chart.

'Yes. I'm okay.' I didn't want to tell her that my rising anger is probably setting her machine off. I don't need any more questions. I'd already fended off the cops' questions by throwing Lachy under the bus. He'd been so aggressive at our final one-on-one session that I knew there was more to his attendance than to just find himself. Never expected him to have planted listening devices and notes in people's rooms though. He really did help me make this work. Or, actually, he really helped Megan. She's lucky I didn't dob her in.

The nurse smiles. 'You need to rest. I'll be back shortly to check these numbers again.' Then she leaves.

'How did you know it was me?' Megan asks, as the door closes.

'You're the only other person getting around the retreat in stilettos. I heard your heels clacking behind me before it went dark.'

'You'll be thanking me soon enough,' she says and her tone is venomous.

I run a hand over the large bandage under my hair. Kitty did a good job of hiding it for the video but I know there'll be a decent scar.

I don't respond to Megan. I just follow the nurse's orders and get some sleep.

Chapter 42

Molly

Two Weeks Later

'Sand & Salt Resort, how can I help you?' I say, answering the phone that has been ringing off the hook for the past fortnight. I pause. 'No, sorry I can't provide a comment at this time. Good-bye.'

I hang up the phone on the hundredth reporter to call the resort since Celia's attack. Thankfully, for every call for a comment there's been a call for a booking too. Sand & Salt is officially booked out for the next twelve months, including a retreat with a well-known health and fitness influencer. For some reason I've agreed to torture myself again.

When Celia went live from her hospital bed last week, she followed it up with several flattering social media posts about her stay with us. It honestly gave proof to the saying not to believe everything you see on the internet. It has pictures of her on the beach, by the pool and watching the sunrise from her balcony. I don't even know when she had a chance to take half of the photos considering I mainly saw her scowling or arguing with guests.

We've been getting bookings for couples who want to relax, for families to have a holiday, for corporates wanting to build staff morale and, unfortunately, for weirdos who just specifically want to stay in Celia's room and are coming for the sole purpose of sleeping in the same place she did. The idea of having more sickos, like Lachy, around here creeps me out but Joey advised me not to turn anyone away.

I definitely couldn't argue with my boss. I'd had to beg him not to fire me when the final retreat guests had left. He jumped on a plane thinking I'd destroyed this place and he wasn't far off the mark. But thanks to Celia's posts, things picked up and Joey learned that all publicity was good publicity. He's hanging around though now, which means he doesn't fully trust me. That's okay. I know I can prove myself. I survived Cyclone Celia.

The door to the reception opens and Greg walks in. His face is red and slicked with sweat.

'That's the last one done,' he says, finding his water bottle behind the desk and taking a large swig.

'That's a relief. Thank you.'

Greg has spent the week working with a security company to install cameras around the resort. We now have a screen monitoring and recording every outdoor area around Sand & Salt. It feels a bit invasive but after everything that's happened, it's necessary.

Greg looks at his watch. 'Three o'clock. Any check-ins today? Want me to stick around?'

'Just one family, I can handle it. You've done heaps. Go home and rest.'

He smiles and heads out the door, calling behind him, 'See ya, mate.'

Greg hasn't been gone five minutes before an enthusiastic family of four burst through the door. The man and woman look to be in their forties and have two teenaged girls in tow. Both girls have their heads down and are mindlessly scrolling on their phones as they enter.

'Welcome to Sand & Salt,' I say, getting up from behind the reception desk.

The girls look up at the sound of my voice and both of their eyes widen.

'Oh my God,' the younger of the two says. 'Are you the boss here?'

'Yeah, like did you meet Celia Marsden?' the other adds.

The younger girl continues before I can answer. 'Will you show us where she stayed? Did she leave any clothes behind?'

I blink rapidly at the questions being fired off at me.

'Girls,' their mother hisses, 'that's extremely inappropriate.' Her tone does not match her words and I get the sense she's saying it out of duty rather than actually wanting her girls to stop prying.

'I did meet Celia,' I say, forcing a smile. 'Let's get you checked in.' I ignore the other questions and get started on their paperwork.

The two girls take the hint and get back to scrolling but not before snapping a selfie of themselves with me in the background.

I want to be annoyed at the invasion of my privacy, at their photographing me without consent but they're not the first to ask questions or take photos in the past fortnight and I can't take anymore drama.

Two weeks ago I thought I was going to be unemployed and homeless. Now I've been given a generous pay rise and have a year of good business ahead of me.

I put on my best smile and lead them to their room.

Chapter 43

Nadia

Three Months Later

'Stop fussing,' Tanner says, as I wipe the kitchen counter clean for the fifth time in the past thirty minutes.

'I'm nervous,' I say. 'Mum will be fine but Dad can be a hard-ass. Especially after what happened with my ex.'

Tanner is meeting my parents tonight. I've been putting it off but I move into Tanner's house next week and over my father's dead body am I living with a man he hasn't met. It's ridiculous considering I've basically lived here since we left the retreat. On the Gold Coast, I was still living with Mum and Dad so I certainly wasn't hosting sleepovers there with my adult boyfriend. When Tanner came down, it was strictly dates in public. No home visits. Therefore, most of our time has been spent here, at his place in Brisbane.

'Relax,' he says, 'I can handle your dad.' He smiles and pulls me into him. I'll never get tired of being held by Tanner. His strong body enveloping mine and taking all my worries and pain away.

Things had moved fast when we left the retreat. Thankfully, the trolls forgot about me quickly and turned to Lachy and the attack. I wanted to put the drama of the weekend behind me and focus on what I'd gained. I was happy, sure. But what I really felt was hope. Hope that I wouldn't be living with my parents, as a thirty-two-year-old divorcee with a criminal record, forever. Hope that there was a second-chance at love for me and that perhaps the husband and kids dream was still alive.

The more time I spent with Tanner the more hopeful I felt. He wanted kids as well. He wanted the "white-picket fence and kicking the footy around in the backyard with the kids" dream too.

One month into our relationship, we got notified that Celia Marsden would be refunding us in full for our retreat and paying us a small amount for the inconvenience. I would say what happened was more than an inconvenience but I was happy to pocket the money. Tanner thinks it was a gesture to thank us for not slagging her off all over social media but as I said, I was more than happy to leave the drama behind.

Now it's been three months, we're about to live together, and I start a job working at the hospital near Tanner's station.

But first, tonight. I let out a sigh, allowing the tension to leave my body as Tanner traces circles on my back.

'Can't we just cancel dinner and stay like this?' I ask, pulling back and looking up into his eyes.

'Nope, because this is the final step before I get to call you my official housemate.' He grins widely.

'Housemate? Sounds so platonic.'

'Housemate with benefits?'

I laugh and push him away, just as the doorbell rings.

'Deep breaths,' Tanner teases, as he walks past me towards the front door.

We open the door, hand in hand and I wonder if this is how the contestants feel on *The Bachelor* during hometown week. Obviously, he's not dating three other girls as well, but the nerves and desperate hope for my family's approval is there and it's making me nauseous.

My mum's excited squeals of hello and the warm hug she immediately pulls Tanner in for eases some of my worries. Then Dad shakes his hand and offers him a half smile. Not a bad start.

Later, when we are seated around Tanner's dining room table, I pour everyone some wine and begin serving dinner.

'Your house is beautiful, Tanner,' my mum gushes, as she takes a sip of her drink.

'Thank you, Mrs Lombardi,' he says.

She gasps. 'That makes me sound old. Call me Fran.'

'Well, Fran.' Tanner smiles. 'How was the trip up?'

'The motorway is a nightmare,' Dad cuts in. 'Took over an hour to get here.'

'Oh, Tony,' Mum says, 'it wasn't that bad.'

I'd been waiting for Dad to comment on how far I'd be moving away. I've never lived further than fifteen minutes from my parents.

'Don't worry, Dad. We'll come down to visit heaps. Plus nothing beats the Gold Coast beaches.'

I place a plate of cannelloni in front of everyone and for a few minutes it's silent as everyone eats.

'Delicious, darling,' Mum says.

'Just like you taught me,' I reply.

Tanner is serving himself and Dad seconds when Mum speaks up.

'Did you hear Celia Marsden is writing another book?'

'Can we not talk about her?' I say, and both Dad and Tanner grunt in agreement.

'Well, I saw it on her Instagram today and I thought it was interesting, that's all,' she says, clearly disappointed that we aren't excited by the news.

'Why do you care anyway?' I ask.

'Well, her first book was so good. And you met her.'

'Mum, she's a psycho bitch. I couldn't stand her. Promise me you won't suggest the new book to your book club.'

Mum rolls her eyes. 'No promises. Besides, her last book found you a beautiful man.'

Tanner's cheeks redden. 'Thank you, Fran.'

'Don't encourage her,' I say, turning to Tanner. 'Even if she's right,' I say a little quieter. There's no denying that Celia's retreat did have some positives.

Dad and Tanner's phones chime an alert at the same time. It's a notification from the football app, I recognise the sound.

Tanner apologises and quickly puts his phone away.

'Don't apologise. Game's starting. Who do you follow?' Dad asks.

'Tigers,' he says.

Dad slaps him on the back. 'Good man. Now where's the TV, let's leave these two to start planning how they'll make this house of yours less bachelor-pad and more Nadia.'

My eyes widen and my heart races. Was that all it took? A mutual love for the same football team.

Then Mum whispers to me. 'He already liked him, you know. We've never seen you so happy and so healthy.'

I smile.

'So,' Mum says. 'I think you need a new kitchen table. This one will not be big enough when the family starts to grow.'

I laugh and take a sip of my wine.

Chapter 44

Jocelyn

Six Months Later

'Joss, what's taking you so long?' Andy calls from the kitchen.

We're heading out for dinner with some friends. I really don't want to but Andy says these things are important for my recovery.

After we left the retreat, we returned to regular life. I kept working in the salon, gossiping away as I styled client after client's hair. Then one day, we received notification that we've been refunded and compensated by Celia Marsden.

It triggered a panic attack. Andy came home from work and found me in a ball in the shower. The water had run cold and I was sitting there rocking back and forth.

That's the night I told Andy what happened. That I'd snuck out of our room and saw Celia get attacked. I told him that every night since, I had nightmares. And that's if I managed to sleep. Most of the time I just lie there, listening for noises. Imagining that same sound of sticks snapping in the bushes and footsteps getting closer.

'I'm coming,' I call back to him. 'I just need five more minutes.'

I stare down at the box in front of me in the bathroom. I've stared at this box a hundred times before. I don't need to read the instructions. I know what to do.

I tear open the plastic and sit on the toilet.

Andy knocks softly on the bathroom door. 'Are you okay?'

'Yep, be out in a sec.'

He's been so good to me since that night. He's always been great but now he's more attentive and caring and sensitive. There has been no pressure on me to get pregnant or even discuss getting pregnant. After that night, he went with me to the doctor and made all the phone calls when I was referred to see a psychiatrist.

I'm getting better. I'm sleeping better, with the help of some tablets the doctor prescribed. But going out at night is hard. I am constantly looking around. Observing everything. It's as though I'm looking for a crime to take place in front of me and I don't want to miss a detail. I felt so guilty for not calling the police and even more guilty not being able to identify Celia's attacker. I was lucky the police didn't charge me for not telling them what I saw straight away. Snippets of the night often come to me and even though Lachy is behind bars, it doesn't sit right. Lachy was a tall guy. The more I replay the scene, the more certain I am that the person who pushed Celia was below average height. I hadn't been able to give the police a description at the time. But the details of the night that keep coming back are more and more clear and I think there's been a mistake. But I have to let it go. I have to let it all go or I will live in this state of fear forever.

I wash my hands and then check my watch. One more minute.

I haven't tracked my ovulation days in six months. I haven't taken my pre-natal vitamins. Andy and I have only been intimate a few times recently because even that has been a trigger. Knowing that Lachy had listened in on us at the retreat has taken the spark and excitement out of sex for me. I'm so paranoid.

But it has happened and now I'm late.

I look at the pregnancy test. Then at the box. Then back at the stick. *No way.*

I open the door of our ensuite. Andy is sitting on the bed and looks up at me as I come out with my hand behind my back.

'You ready to go?' he says.

'Yep,' I say. 'But it'll be just water for me tonight.'

He narrows his eyes at me and I smile, holding up the positive pregnancy test for him to see.

'What?' he asks, jumping to his feet.

'I'm pregnant,' I say.

He picks me up and spins me around, before kissing me firmly on the lips. Then he pulls back. 'And you're okay? You want this?'

I nod, tears rolling down my cheeks. 'Yes, more than anything.' And I mean it.

Chapter 45

Celia

One Year Later

I twirl in front of the mirror and smile. *Perfect.* Today is the first day of my book tour and I need to look the part. This isn't just a tour for my new book. It is the tour for the new Celia. Just as stylish as ever but now with a greater purpose. Well, at least that's what I've advertised and companies throw money at me for doing so, so I don't care what I have to fake.

The new Celia is battling trolls one keyboard warrior at a time. In reality, I couldn't care less what people think of me. As long as I am making sales and gaining followers, I am happy. But what everyone else sees is me promoting mental health, social media education and tougher laws regarding social media. Hell, I could probably run for council and get elected at this point. I am hot.

'Celia,' Tom calls from downstairs. He should've taken the kids to their sports by now. I don't want their dirty breakfast hands touching me in this outfit. 'Can you come down here?'

I carefully take the stairs in my brand new Valentino boots and find Tom in the kitchen studying his computer screen.

When he sees me, he waves me over to look at the screen. 'What is this payment?'

It was money I'd sent to Lachy. I'd reimbursed all the guests of my retreat and given a little extra to those who had received notes. I wouldn't call it hush money but if it was an incentive to keep their lips sealed about the weekend, it had worked. I had to reimburse him too. It seemed the right thing to do. And scratched away just a teeny bit of the guilt I was feeling about framing him, even if he was a total creep and not entirely innocent.

I know Tom won't be happy about me paying my attacker. Well, the guy he believes is my attacker.

I purse my lips together, trying to look as though I'm thinking.

'It's a BPAY payment to Corrective Services NSW,' he clarifies. 'What's it for?'

Shit. Shit. Shit. Why is he even studying our bank account? We have plenty of money—thanks to me, I might add.

'I'm not sure,' I say. 'But I had to pay quite a few random places while writing the new book. You know, research and whatever.'

'Hmm, yeah fair enough,' he says and I hope that's the end of it.

'Kitty's picking me up in five. I'll be at the signing all day.'

Kitty and I had actually co-written the new book, *Hacking the Mind of the Keyboard Warrior*. It was a deep dive into the psychology of online bullies and unfortunately, I had to admit that my skills as a psychologist had been lacking. I'd let it slip by not practising and not undertaking professional development. I needed someone who was constantly learning still and that was Kitty. There is still unspoken tension between us but we've produced a beauty of a book, and it's a bestseller.

A car honks from outside and I call goodbye to Tom and the kids who are now rushing to pack sports gear and drink bottles into backpacks.

My hand aches as I sign what must be the hundredth copy of *Hacking the Mind of the Keyboard Warrior*.

Megan rushes up to us. I still burn with anger at the sight of her. I'd wanted to fire her but she knew the truth. We could both ruin each other. This way was better for both of us.

'You're almost done ladies,' she says, in a way that makes me think Kitty and I are runners in a marathon and she's our pep-talking coach. It did feel like a marathon in a way. Hours we've been sitting here meeting readers, making small talk and signing their book before politely hurrying them along.

I'd done this for *Loveless Marriage* and I had to admit it was much more enjoyable with Kitty by my side.

A woman with dark hair approaches Kitty and there are only a handful of people behind her. Home stretch. Kitty signs her book before she places it in front of me to do the same.

I scribble my signature, my hand basically working off muscle memory alone at this point and then smile and hand it back to the woman.

She leans in close and whispers, 'I know what you did at the retreat.' Then she rushes away and is lost to the crowd, who are now enjoying refreshments.

I inhale sharply and lean over to Kitty. 'Who was that?'

Kitty looks at me. 'Who?'

'That last book you signed—who'd you make it out to?'

She narrows her eyes for a moment, thinking. She's written personalised messages for so many people today. 'Her name was Louisa. Louisa Manningham. So weird she wanted her last name too.' Kitty laughs, totally unaware of who the woman was.

My mouth goes dry and I look back in the direction the woman had walked in but she's long gone—with my book and my secret.

Acknowledgements

Firstly, thank you to my readers for taking the time to read *The Retreat.* Writing has introduced me to a wonderful world of readers and fellow writers, who are so supportive and encouraging, and I'm grateful for all of you.

Thank you to Mel Noorderbroek for editing my work and to The Cover Collection for the beautiful cover.

Thanks Jacqui and Emma for being my beta readers and giving me the confidence to get this book out into the world. Thank you Bec for reading *The Retreat* several times and for never letting me quit.

Thanks Emma, Elle and Ali who still give me a hit of energy and laughter everyday.

Thank you Madds and Josh for your expertise and for your inspiration as first responders in real-life.

Finally, thank you to my husband for your support and for making this all possible for me.

About the Author

Stephanie Hazeltine is a contemporary fiction author who writes about fearless females as they fall in love, navigate motherhood or tackle mysteries.
She lives in Melbourne with her husband, two kids and two cavoodles.

GET IN TOUCH
Website: www.stephaniehazeltine.com
Instagram: @stephaniehazeltinewrites
TikTok: @stephaniehazeltinewrites

Also By Stephanie Hazeltine

Suburban Secrets Series - Domestic Thriller/Women's Fiction

While the Baby Sleeps

(Available in eBook and Paperback)

You Weren't Watching

(Available in eBook and Paperback)

Romance

Anyone But Him - a spicy collection of novellas

(Available in eBook and Paperback)

All I Want for Chris-mas - a spicy collection of novellas

(Available in eBook and Paperback)

Printed in Great Britain
by Amazon

38937887R00131